The Magisterium

Introducing the Nikolaitans

By Lew White

PRINTED VERSION

**Both printed and ebooks are available at Amazon
Search for other books by author Lew White**

The MAGISTERIUM
Introducing the Nikolaitans

Copyright © 2021 Lew White

In the ebook version, links are active.
Watch a youtube video excerpt describing this book:
https://youtu.be/MoVoQWvBmRc

CONTENTS

Introduction

The Tetragrammaton Written in Bedrock

A life-sized print of the *Los Lunas Stone* is used as a back-drop in many videos on Lew White's youtube channel. It is known as the Decalogue Stone, and is located at Hidden Mountain near Los Lunas, New Mexico in the USA. The inscription it bears is the Ten Commandments, and it was etched almost 3000 years ago to serve as a gatestone to one of the colonies of the **sea empire** of king Shalomoh. The authentic *Hebrew script* is on this stone.

In the Writing of Truth, the Name is the Stone the builders rejected (Psalm 118:26). Yahusha called it the *key of knowledge*, which had been rejected by the teachers, and withheld from the people.
They did not know the NAME of their Creator.
In May of 2008, a new dogma was announced.
The pope of Rome made the *utterance* of the Name prohibited in public prayer, songs, and worship.
Many have submitted to the authority of the teachings of the Nikolaitans.
Here in the last days, Yahusha is raising up His Natsarim to announce the Truth..
We are Yahusha's ambassadors, and we are reappearing in the last days to announce His Reign is drawing near.

Magisterium, a Latin word for *teaching authority*, points to the most powerful human organization controlling doctrines. The Greek word is Didascalia. It is given authority by the dragon. *The dragon pursues the offspring of the wife of Yahuah; those guarding the Commandments of Alahim and holding to the testimony of Yahusha* (Rev. 12:17). Masquerading as messengers of light, the dragon's servants teach lawlessness and traditions inherited from paganism. The Magisterium admits the head of this organization is a *vicar*, standing in the place of another.

THE FOURTH BEAST IS ROME
It's the final echelon of the ancient World Order

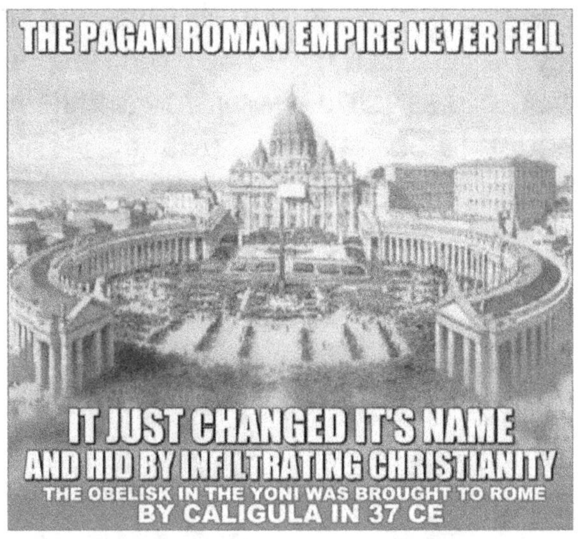

Rome's giant shivalingam / yoni is on display for all to see, but the Nikolaitans have blinded the eyes of the people. What was whispered in secret is now being revealed. Esoteric symbols and practices are being exposed. The obelisk shown in this photo was brought to Rome from Egypt by Caligula in 37 CE.

A New Reign is coming.
It will be here on Earth, and the *reign of Babel* will fall to the *Reign of Yahusha*. (See Revelation 11:15)

Yahusha revealed things in the 17th chapter of Yahukanon (aka John). His true followers were, and still are, very different from the followers of the dragon. Consider what Yahusha said at verse 6:

"I have revealed Your Name to the men whom You gave Me out of the world. They were Yours, and You gave them to Me, and they have guarded Your Word."

This statement alludes to the fact that *most people will not know the Name*, and their teachers have intentionally *hidden* it. It is the key of knowledge. His treasured possession *meditates* on His Name, and they speak to one another (Malaki 3:16-18).

INTRODUCING THE NIKOLAITANS

A full range of peer abuse, mobbing, and intimidation suggest to us a similar word: *bullying*. The *"conquers of the people"* [NIKO+LAITY] is the literal meaning of the word *Nikolaitans*.

All Nikolaitans are religious bullies. They project an air of entitlement. They amass in groups with descriptive labels, often using the names of their founders, and impose their authority over any willing to let them. They often name their "ministry" after themselves or a location, not Yahusha.

They endow *orders* from their own peers in a process called *ordination*. They bear titles, hats, and costumes that allow them to be distinguished from each other, and other groups. They are divisive, not unifying. They consider themselves in charge over the sheep. They control teachings, and guide us into confusion. Yahusha said He hates them. (Rev. 2:6)

MYSTAGOGUES

Nikolaitanes conquer the common people in all kinds of ways. They are doctrinal controllers who decide what teachings are disseminated into the pure, empty minds of their audience. The pagan world is still all around us, camouflaged under the customs. Exoteric (outsider perceptions) of widely popular customs only reveal a small hint of the true origin and meaning behind them. The outside view of the customs are displayed in plain sight in every grocery and retailer as the seasonal decorations make their rounds. The hidden meaning of them is known to the mystagogues. The esoteric knowledge of the real meaning is kept from the masses. Mystagogues in the ancient world trained their adherents in the mysteries through a series of graded levels as they slowly revealed esoteric secrets, much as we see done over many years in Masonic Lodges. Perhaps the greatest objective of the mystagogues was to conceal the real name of their deities. They believed if an enemy knew the names of their deities, they would be used against them. They rendered the names of their deities into cryptograms, and often used fake names that only a few knew how to decode. This was the practice adopted in the case of the substitute terms for the Name of Yahusha. In the Eastern Roman Empire, they used the christogram **IC-XC** in place of the Name. In the Western Roman Empire, they used the christogram **IHS**.

The ancient Egyptians used a bar above or below the name of their deities to designate that the writing represented the name of a deity. We see this practice is expressed in their cartouches. The bar is referred to as a *titlos* (title bar). This mystagogue trait is seen in the Latin Vulgate's rendering of the Name of Yahusha: <u>**IESV**</u>. Those who know what they are looking at will realize this was brought into the first edition of the Authorized Version, or KJV. Here's a close-up photo of the 1st edition of the KJV showing how the Anglican Catholics copied the encrypted christogram with the *titlos* and **exact spelling** taken directly from the Latin Vulgate:

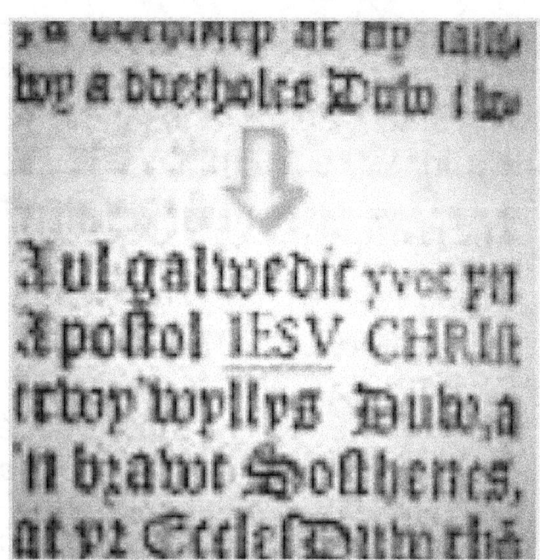

<u>IESV</u> is only an encryption that slowly evolved into *JESUS*.

Is The KJV A Good Translation?

The KJV omits the Name and inserts the device LORD (from the *Latin Vulgate's* "Dominus"), from which it was translated into English.

At Acts 12:4, the KJV is the only translation using the word EASTER for Pascha / Pesak, which in 27 other instances the word *Passover* is correctly used. EASTER is the Earth Mother, aka Eostre, or Ishtar.

At Mt. 26:17, "on the first day of unleavened bread" (the 15th day of the 1st month), the KJV states the students of Yahusha were speaking to Him about where to prepare the Passover (which is the 14th, the day Yahusha was placed on the stake). Yahusha was in the tomb on the first day of unleavened bread. This mistake was inherited by the NIV, NASB, and most other English translations. The BYNV has these error corrected. How could men holding doctorates in theology possibly err so blatantly, unless their credentials would be marred? Do such men not fear Yahuah?

TEST YOUR TRANSLATIONS

One of many ways to test any translation is at Mt. 26:17.

If a translation states "On the first day of Matsah" in the opening words, that source has inherent errors in it. It reads incorrectly in the Peshitta, Cepher, AENT, NIV, NASB, 1599 Geneva, 1611 KJV, and many other highly respected translations.

How does your preferred text read at Mt. 26:17?

If the first Natsarim were talking to Yahusha about where to prepare for the Pesak *on the first day of Matsah*, they would be needing more education about talking to the dead, and a time machine.

Pesak is on the 14th, and the first day of Matsah is the 15th of the first month. Yahusha's body was hurried into the borrowed tomb before the first day of Matsah. The Christian translations all follow the same errors of the Latin Vulgate.
They do not yet know about the redemption plan nor follow the festivals of Yahuah.
Look inside the BYNV:
https://www.amazon.com/gp/product/B00EAB3U9I/ref=dbs_a_def_rwt_hsch_vapi_taft_p1_i8

A BYNV helps both beginners and scholars understand what Yahusha wants to say in the jabbering lip and foreign language He told us He would speak to His people, and that time is now.

Confute The Error Of The Mystagogues
Read their Preface to them (examples below).
BEL (Baal) means LORD. Other forms meaning LORD are Aduni, Kurios, Dominus. All of these are substitutes for the true Name, YAHUAH. Most prefaces will explain they replaced it with their "device" due to tradition. The priests of Bel were shown their error at Mt. Karmal (by AliYahu) and the crowds finally shouted, "Yahuah! He is Alahim!" (1Kings 18). Like our fathers before us, we have forgotten Yahuah's Name for BEL (YirmeYahu 23:27).

I WAS TAUGHT BY JESUITS

In several of my books there is an admission that I was taught by the best educators this planet has ever known, the **_Jesuits_** (aka, Jesuit-Illuminati). They educate the children of upwardly-mobile politicians and businessmen to prepare them for future leaders within the clergy, or as operatives within governments and industry when they are older.

These schools are openly called *"prep-schools."* This order was founded by Inigo Loyola (a Spanish soldier turned priest) in 1534 with the prime directive of restoring authoritarian power to the papacy. The papacy had lost that authority as a result of the nobles turning away during the Reformation.

The Societas IESV was established as a militant order, the Counter-Reformation, to use any and all means necessary, even assassination, to bring governments under their influence. The Jesuit general is the real head of the Roman Circus. Regimini militantis Ecclesiae was the papal bull promulgated by Pope Paul III on September 27, 1540, which gave a first approval to the Society of Jesus.

Look up the *Jesuit Oath of Induction* if you are interested in how far they will go to achieve their goals. The whole objective is control over the people.

The Jesuits knew that the path to restoring power was through the children of the Nobility, so they became educators. Ignatius Loyola founded the Jesuit order, and quoted Aristotle with the words, *"Give me a child until he is seven, and I will show you the man."*

Essentially, this is mind-controlling psychotherapy, and it took Yahusha to snap me out of it.

What About The Protestants?

All of theses are fractured offspring of the Roman Catholic Magisterium, beginning with the Eastern Orthodox schism over political and theological differences (1053-1054). The divisions are so numerous, what was confusing before has exponentially exploded and galloped around the world. When we study and obey the Ten Commandments, we grow away from men and very close to the heart of Yahuah. This causes the world to hate us. They hate us because they hated Yahusha first. Natsarim are the branches of Yahusha, and He is our Teacher. He interprets His Word to us. We trust no human teaching authorities, they lead us away from obeying Yahusha.

Belief, without *obedience,* is dead belief.

When someone says, *"I know Him,"* but does not *obey* His Commandments, 1 Yn. 2:4 calls that person a liar, and the Truth is not in him. Those who guard and teach the Commandments are truly Yahusha's students, and they know the Truth.
His yoke (teachings, orders, Commandments) are easy and light.
The yoke of men is heavy with steeples, buildings, domes, re-invented pagan festivals of fertility camouflaged under new meanings, Sunday (Sun worship), liturgies, training in disobedience and believing someone else obeyed for them, dispensationalism, Marcionism, replacement theology, and the lack of a Passover are all indicators that there is a great deal wrong.
We are to walk as Yahusha walked, not walk like an *Egyptian*. The Catechetical School at Alexandria is the hatching point from which all Christianities sprang from. *That snake pit is in Egypt.* It moved one of it's obelisks to Rome. Even demons believe that Yahuah is Yahusha; and they tremble.

Some ancient Nimrod architechure passed-down from mystagogues is esoteric (hidden) sexual imagery hiding in plain sight. The common outsider only sees the exoteric understanding, not perceiving the Shivalingams they represent.

IMAGE OF THE BEAST

The symbol of the crux became the universal symbol of Christianity under Constantine.
It was already the symbol of His Sun deity.
Sun worship was universalized during the reign of Constantine. His creed is quoted below, and he ended it with his curse. The dragon poisoned the waters (people) by mixing-in familiar symbols & customs. Sun-day, trinities, cruxes, pillars, haloes, statues, holy water, and prayers to the dead using beads and candles originate with Hinduism.

TORAH INSTITUTE

CONSTANTINE'S CREED:

"I renounce all customs, rites, legalisms, unleavened breads and sacrifices of lambs of the Hebrews, and all the other festivals of the Hebrews, sacrifices, prayers, aspirations, purifications, sanctifications, and propitiations, fasts and new moons, Sabbaths, superstitions, hymns and chants, observances. and assemblies. Absolutely everything Yahudi, every law, rite, and custom, and if afterwards I shall wish to deny and return to Yahudim superstition, or shall be found eating with Yahudim, or feasting with them, or secretly conversing and condemning the Christian religion instead of openly confuting them and condemning their vain faith, then let the trembling of Cain and the leprosy of Gehazi cleave to me, as well as the legal punishments to which I acknowledge myself liable. And may I be an anathema in the world to come, and may my soul be set down with satan and the devils."

Natsarim wishing to join this "holy community" were compelled to adopt a different set of rules and customs. All new members were to take this oath:

"I accept all customs, rites,
legalism, and feasts of the
Romans' sacrifices. Prayers,
purifications with water,
sanctifications by Pontificus Maximus (high priest of Rome), propitiations, and feasts, and the New Sabbath Dies Solis (Day of the Sun), all new chants and observances, and all the foods and drinks of the Romans. I absolutely accept everything Roman, every new law, rite and custom, of Rome, and the New Roman Religion."

In approximately 365 AD, the Council of Laodicea made all Natsarim anathema:

"Christians must not Judaize by resting on the Sabbath, but must work on that day. Rather, honoring the Lord's Day.
But if any shall be found to be Judaizers, let them be anathema (separated) from Christ."

NOTE:

Protestants are included as they still observe the holidays and SUN-day of Rome.

Sun temples are found in all parts of the world. The Celts called the Sun "GOTT," the word commonly used today as a Teutonic morphism of the first Sun deity, Nimrod. Solar deities are all based on the 1st

king of Babel.
The CROSS is the IMAGE of the solar deity throughout history.
The DAY OF THE SUN has been the MARK on the beast people, and the Catholic circus openly claims it as their mark of authority to change one of the Ten Commandments (they've changed more than one). The riddle is not solvable without wisdom, so to reject the Commandments takes away their ability to possess wisdom. The riddle is offered to us at Revelation 13 . . . . those buying and selling do not discern the day of rest, but think it is SUN-day. Those who know Yahusha guard His Commandments, 1 Yn. 2:4-7.
Examine the photos above, and ask yourself if Yahusha would ever guide His followers to bow to images, talk to the dead, or receive the image of the Roman solar deity placed on their heads.
"If anyone worships the beast and his image, and receives his mark upon his forehead or upon his hand, he also shall drink of the wine of the wrath of Yahuah, which is poured out undiluted into the cup of His wrath." - see Rev. 14:9-10
"According to Prescott, when the Spaniards first arrived in Mexico, they were shocked to behold the CROSS, the sacred emblem of their own Catholic faith, reverenced in Aztec temples." (excerpt, Sunday Origins)
There is a Sun temple called the "Temple of the Cross" in Palenque, Mexico founded in the ninth-century BCE. Aztec Sun temples were built as giant altars where human sacrifices were offered to the Sun. "In this sign conquer" was the message given to Constantine in his battle against Maxentius in 312 CE. Constantine

worshipped Apollo, the Sun.

Why People Get Upset When They Hear Truth
Watch a video on Lew White's YouTube channel:
COGNITIVE DISSONANCE
(picture is linked in the eBook version):

The Masses Have Been Programmed
To begin, let's look at the meaning of some words:
Therapy: treatment
Psycho: mind
Systemic: pervasive, inherent, shared within a system, affecting or connected to the whole.

Systemic therapy in the psychotherapeutic sense concerns treating large groups of people and their relationships among one another, and dealing with their interactions among other groups.
To be effective, therapy is conducted with regularity to train, control, and monitor the progress of those under treatment. Christian pastors are trained to think apologetically in defense of their traditional views, and transfer those views into large masses of people who trust in their skills, because people typically do not study on their own.
Psychology is the study of mental processes.

People who go to a steeple every week in the morning have been programmed by trained psychotherapists called pastors. When they hear the Truth spoken to them, their programming conflicts with it, and they experience mental stress, or dissonance (inconsistencies between one's actions and beliefs). Here's the definition:

Cognitive Dissonance (Wikipedia quote):

"In the field of psychology, cognitive dissonance occurs when a person holds contradictory beliefs, ideas, or values, and is typically experienced as psychological stress when they participate in an action that goes against one or more of them. According to this theory, when two actions or ideas are not psychologically consistent with each other, people do all in their power to change them until they become consistent. The discomfort is triggered by the person's belief clashing with new information perceived, wherein they try to find a way to resolve the contradiction to reduce their discomfort.

In *A Theory of Cognitive Dissonance* (1957), Leon Festinger proposed that human beings strive for internal psychological consistency to function mentally in the real world. A person who experiences internal inconsistency tends to become psychologically uncomfortable and is motivated to reduce the cognitive dissonance. They tend to make changes to justify the stressful behavior, either by adding new parts to the cognition causing the psychological dissonance (*rationalization*) or by avoiding circumstances and contradictory information likely to increase the magnitude of the cognitive dissonance (*confirmation bias*)."

Paul speaks to this condition in the terms of his time

at 2 Korinthians 10:3-5. The cognitive dissonance in his day was referred to as a stronghold, which we Natsarim are appearing today to tear-down.

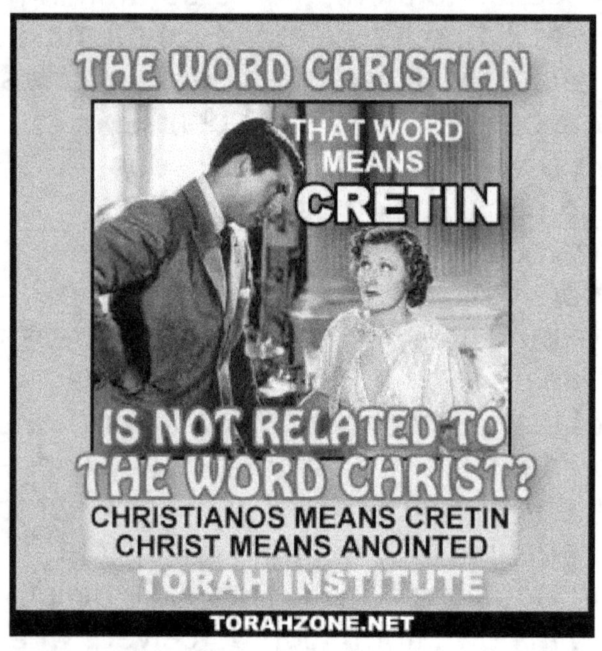

WORD CONTROL BY EDICT

A papal bull (official dogma) issued in 2008 specifically bans the use of the Name in worship, song, or public prayer. It ordered that any forms based on the Tetragrammaton never be uttered as has been the long-held tradition of the Yahudim. The Name is to be *substituted* with other words such as Dominus or LORD.

This bull openly forbids the utterance of the true Name, and it violates the eternal Covenant.

The first, second, and third Commandments are vital for us to know the one we serve, and they tell us that Yahuah is jealous. The papal bull seeks to destroy the Name.

The controversy at Mt. Karmel between the priests of BEL and AliYahu is once again on display for the whole world to witness.

It's **Yahusha**, not ***JEZUS***, who delivers us.

In 2008, the papal bull outlawed the utterance of the Name of Yahuah, and any transliterations based on the Tetragrammaton. The controversy at Mt. Karmel is still before us (1 Kings 18). Some words are literally derived from heathens, adopted from the names for their deities. Examples are GOD (GOTT), Bible (Byblia), Easter (Ishtar), and the names used for the days of the week (Sun Day, Moon Day, Tyr's Day, Woden's Day, Thor's Day, Frigga Day).

The term *grace* refers to the three *graces*, the three daughters of Zeus and Oceanus. The names of pagan deities are forbidden to be uttered on our lips (Ex. 23, Ps. 16).

The Egyptian deity *Amon Ra* is not being called on by the word AMAN (or amen), although mystagogues everywhere may say so. Foreign languages' names for their idols have no connection with Hebrew words. This argument is *non-sequitur*. If a conclusion is "non-sequitur," it does not logically follow the previous argument or statement.

The listener may not realize their teacher is repeating an error without fact-checking it.

The term of affirmation, AMAN (truly), as well as

AMANAH (trustworthy), are clean words in the Eberith language, but sound similar to the Egyptian deity AMON RA. The association of *homonyms* from foreign languages are not violations because they are removed from their proper *contexts*. Many silly arguments do not follow sound reason. The word *faith* is from the Latin word *FIDES*, and relates more to *thought* than *active obedience*. This is the difference in the Greek *mindset* (thought-based) and the Eberith / Hebrew *mindset* (action-based). Yaqub 2:18-26 explains this difference:
"But someone might say, 'you have belief, and I have works.' Show me your belief without your works, and I will show you my belief by my works. You believe Alahim is one. You do well. The demons believe also, and shudder! But do you wish to know, foolish man, that the belief without the works is dead? Was not Abrahim our father declared right by works when he offered Yitshaq his son on the altar? Do you see that the belief was working with his works, and by the works the belief was perfected? . . . You see then that a man is declared right by works, and not by belief alone."
(see full text at Yaqub 2:18-26)

Natsarim Announce Yahusha's Second Coming
Everyone born into this reign of Babel is entangled in a web of strange deceptions. Shatan is the king of Babel. The Writing of Truth calls this fallen one "the dragon."
When the Truth comes along, it sounds ridiculous to them, and they respond with "you're in a cult."
The world is under the influence of mystagogues (interpreters of secrets) and nikolaitans (conquerors of the common people). The world order is the

clergy-nobility-laity power structure controlling teachings.

The traditions and rules of men will not survive the coming reign of Yahusha, and Natsarim are here to tell them. BARUK HABA BASHEM YAHUAH (Psalm 118:26 / Mt. 23:39) means, *"Blessed is the One Who comes in the Name of Yahuah."*

Yahuah is Yahusha, the Living Word, our Deliverer. YAHUSHA means *"I am your Deliverer."*

Be immersed calling on His Name, and obey the Commandments, and He will seal you for the day of our redemption.

One of the dragon's major entanglements is:

SACRAMENTS

When did "sacraments" get invented?

They appeared when the Magisterium made them up.

The doctrines of men have completely taken over the whole world, and the Commandments of Yahuah have been maligned as being obsolete. (see 2 Peter 2:2). The Magisterium has invented its own way, setting itself above the authority of the Writing of Truth.

Yahusha did not come to do-away with His Commandments.

He came to overcome the works of the devil: **Disobedience.**

YOD-HAY-UAU-HAY
Letters read from right-to-left:

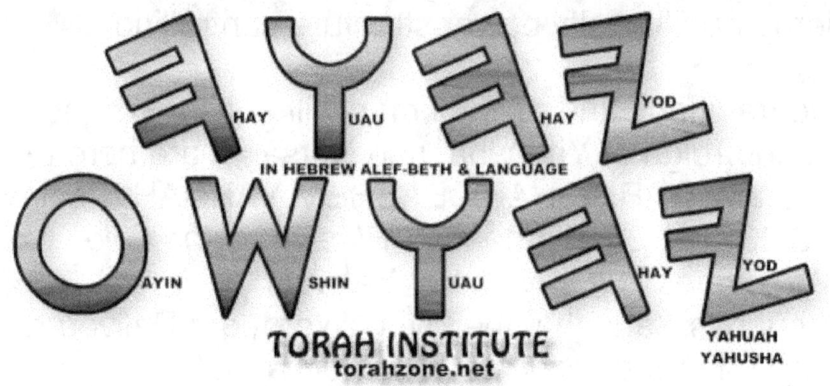

Learn The Parable Of The Fig Tree
"When its branches bud and its leaves begin to sprout, you know that summer is near." - Mt. 24:32
Both men and women are now actively spreading the true message, so let's encourage them to do so. Let the body of Yahusha work together.
"I am the *Vine*, you are the *Natsarim*." - Yn. 15:5
The stones are crying out the Name the builders rejected long ago.

When Yahusha comes, all complaining will cease, and we will stand in awe at the sight of His wounds. We will understand that we, His Own household, put them there. Eternal Life, and what Yahusha said about it, involves abandoning everything taught by men, and embracing the ways we've been taught to ignore, and even abhor.

The way of life is a light yoke, but overcoming the resistance of the world around us is our greatest obstacle. Following Yahusha draws persecution from the world, but those who endure to the end will be delivered. The Information Age is all around us, yet most are drowning in the ignorance of the past.

HOW TORAH BECAME TOXIC

Antiochus Epiphanes had attempted to eliminate all behavior associated with Yahuah's Torah in the 2nd century BCE, forcing the people to eat swine flesh, ignore the 7th day rest, annual appointments, or even possessing and reading the Scriptures. During the reign of Vespasian, the Fiscus Judaicus (a Roman tax on those who practiced Yahuah's Commandments) began in the first century after the destruction of the Temple in Yerusalem in 70 CE. When something is taxed, you get less of it. Constantine's Edict in 321, and his Creed, express a vicious hatred of Yahuah's instructions, and we will examine these things later in this book.

The Alexandrian culture became fixed at the Council of Nicea in 325 CE under Constantine. If you're in this world breathing air, you are surrounded by people who have inhaled **toxic teachings**. TORAH is a Hebrew word meaning teaching. It is identical in meaning to the Latin word "doctrine". The question is, which "torah" is toxic? It may be **Yahuah's Torah**, or men's torah; but you should test which "torah" you are hearing before you take it into your vessel (heart, inner lamp). Commonly the word Torah is translated into the

English word law. We live in a highly deceptive world under the influence of an enemy called the dragon (serpent).

The teaching or training we see conducted through those who appear pious are guiding the masses away from obedience to the Torah of Yahuah. Some have been heard saying the Torah of Yahuah is **"toxic faith."** If one takes the perspective of the dragon, the Torah of Yahuah would be toxic faith.

SUPERSESSIONISM

This is the concept that Christians in the "New Covenant" era replace, supplant, and take over the former identity of Yisharal (Israel). They usurp the promises and leave behind the moral obligations. Some call this *replacement theology*. It's a kind of identity movement. Its ideas originated in the incubator of Christianity at Alexandria, Egypt.

The church fathers at this **Didascalia** or Catechetical School at Alexandria taught that all the promises made to Yisharal were now **inherited** by the Christian Church. The Covenants with Abrahim, Mosheh, and Daud are considered annulled.

This church / circus was [and is] the centralized hierarchy holding all authority over doctrine.

It wields great power because it is the ***1st estate***, (the *clergy*), to which the other two estates must submit (the *Nobility* & *laity*).

Paul warned us about false teachers.

"Now the goal of this command is love from a clean heart, from a good conscience and a sincere belief, which some, having missed the goal, turned aside to senseless talk, wishing to be teachers of Turah, understanding neither what they say nor concerning what they strongly affirm. And we know that the Turah is good if one uses it legitimately, knowing this: that Turah is not laid down for an obedient one, but for the lawless and unruly, for the wicked and for sinners, for the lawless-doers and profane, for those who kill their fathers or mothers, for murderers, for those who whore, for arsenkoites [sodomites], for kidnappers, for liars, for perjurers, and for whatever else that is contrary to sound teaching, according to the esteemed Besorah of the blessed Yahuah which was entrusted to me." (1 Timothy 1:5-11 BYNV)

Teaching authorities today demand the tithe that once supported the old priesthood, yet do not teach obedience to the Ten Commandments. They often claim the Commandments were "done-away," yet only animal blood for atonement has ended along with that old priesthood that collected the tithe that supported them (see Dt. 31:26 & Heb. 8:13).

Yahusha said, "I am the Vine; you are the Natsarim" at Yahukanon (John) 15:5.

Yahusha told His first Natsarim to teach all nations the Name and to obey everything He commanded us to obey. Today, the masses are fed wormwood (altered words) producing lawlessness. The lies are fed to them in steeple places (forbidden to build at Uyiqara / Leviticus 26), and they follow the traditions of men formerly practiced by pagans. They will not receive correction, so Yahuah tightens their chains. Yahusha's Name is not JESUS, ISA, IHS, IESV, or IESOUS. Why would Yahusha be wrathful toward those who know Him by His real Name, and live by every Word that proceeds from the mouth of Yahuah? The dragon is enraged at those who obey (guard, live by) the Commandments of Alahim, and testify of Yahusha (Rev. 12:17). The inhabitants of the Earth will be burned on the Day of Yahuah because they have broken the everlasting Covenant (YashaYahu / Isaiah 24, Mt. 24).

The prophet YirmeYahu (Jer.) is quoted at Hebrews 8 & 10, giving us insight into what is meant concerning the Covenant. It is the same Covenant, "renewed" in men's hearts rather than written in stone as the former was. Before proceeding with this study, please read the entire chapter of YirmeYahu 31. You will immediately recognize how far adrift the church fathers were in their identity of Yisharal, and Yahuah's promises.

Galatians chapter 3:21-26 is misunderstood by the Alexandrian Cult. The **school master** is the **trainer** that directed the details for the offering of animal blood for **sins**.

The trainer was "over us" until Yahusha came to put an end to the animal offerings. The trainer had to exist to point the way to the **final offering** that would "supersede" all other offerings. This same "tutor" also trained us **to know what our offenses are**.

The animal blood covered sins only temporarily; but Yahusha's blood redeems completely:

"Is the Torah then against the promises of Yahuah? Let it not be! For if a law had been given that was able to **make alive**, truly **righteousness** would have been by Torah. *[Animal blood temporarily covered sin, and was never a path to eternal life].*

But the Scripture has shut up all mankind under sin, that the promise by belief in Yahusha Mashiak might be given to those who believe. But before belief came, we were being guarded under Torah, having been shut up for the **belief** being about to be revealed. [Yahusha's blood]

Therefore the Torah became our **trainer** to Mashiak, in order to be declared right by **belief**. And after **belief** has come, we are no longer under a **trainer**. For you are all sons of Yahuah through belief in Mashiak Yahusha." Gal. 3:21-26

Paul uses the word "Torah" to refer to the prescribed decrees that ceremonially covered the sins of the nation. There is confusion because the same word is used to refer to the **moral** instructions which **define** sin for us. If the definition for sin has been annulled, then we can ignore the Ten Commandments entirely. The word "law" or better, **Torah**, refers to the teachings of Yahuah that **train** us in how to **love** Him and one another.

THE SCHOOL MASTER
When Torah is violated, we fail to love, so we have sinned. To atone, animal blood was offered.
The **trainer** that brought us to Yahusha was the Torah concerning **animal sacrifices**.
The same word, Torah, is used to apply to the instructions for atoning for sin. Before Yahusha offered His Own blood, trust had to be in the **atoning blood of animals** in shadows performed by priests. Now we trust in the **object** that cast the shadows: **Yahusha's blood**.
The trainer (or school master) Paul is speaking of in Galatians concerns the former procedures using animal blood. Paul is misunderstood by those who are untrained in the belief. Remember, the Galatians never had the Torah, but were falling back into their former pagan practices. Their *special days* were not Yahuah's Shabath and festivals, but were their former *weak and miserable heathen* activities now

adopted by Christianity. Have you noticed Halloween, Sun-day, pillars and bells, Valentine's Day, making cakes to make wishes, or asked a pastor if Yahusha was really born on December 25th?

Another perspective of our instruction, or Torah-training, involves that which *defines sin* for us. What we learn to be sin through the Torah is also taught to us by the trainer, the Torah.
The school master teaches the young learner to live properly. The Torah is the school master.
When the student has **learned** what the school master has taught, it's time for the student to put what has been learned into practice. If the student thinks what he **learned** from the school master may be forgotten, he has been deluded.
The one that has learned no longer needs a school master, if they **practice** what they have learned. The Torah teaches us how to love Yahuah, and one another. It will produce the **behavior** (fruit) Yahusha expects of us. The only fruit Yahusha is looking for is our obedience.

YAHUAH'S TORAH IS NOT TOXIC
A few years ago, as I listened to my radio while driving home from work, a Christian preacher was teaching against the "works of the law."
He said the TORAH IS TOXIC, and must be kept far from a Christian's walk. He expressed this in a tone of disgust, as if the words were bitter in his mouth.
Teachers who are held captive to the Alexandrian Cult understand "works of the law" to refer to **obeying** the Commandments, which they call **"legalism."**
The *works of the law* spoken of in Scripture at

Romans 3:28 & Galatians 2:16 pertain to the atonement provided by the offering of *animal blood* for sin, a shadow or pattern that pointed to the ultimate offering: the precious blood of Yahusha. **Yahuah's Torah is not toxic.**
Read Psalm 1:1-6: "Contented is the man who shall not walk in the counsel of the wrong, and shall not stand in the path of sinners, and shall not sit in the seat of scoffers, But **his delight** is in the **Torah of Yahuah**, and he meditates in His Torah yom and lailah. For he shall be as a tree planted by the rivers of water, that yields its fruit in its season, And whose leaf does not wither, and whatever he does prospers. The wrong are not so, but are like the chaff which the wind blows away.
Therefore the wrong shall not rise in the judgment, Nor sinners in the assembly of the righteous. ForYahuah knows the way of the righteous, but the way of the wicked ones will perish." [see also Ps. 119]

The teachings of men are highly toxic, since they reject the things that produce loving-kindness and right behavior.
The Torah is perfect: Psalm 19:7-10:
"The Torah of **Yahuah** is perfect, bringing back the being; the witness of **Yahuah** is trustworthy, making wise the simple; the orders of **Yahuah** are straight, rejoicing the heart; the command of Yahuah is clear, enlightening the eyes; the fear of Yahuah is clean, standing forever; the right-rulings of Yahuah are true, They are righteous altogether, more desirable than gold, than much fine gold; and sweeter than honey and the honeycomb."

Supersessionists teach whatever helps them, such

as obligatory tithing to them at obligatory weekly *services*. They take-on the role of the obsolete priesthood set up under the former pattern of the school master, and recite texts out of context to make circumstances appear to be something they are not. For example, they may quote this:

Gal 6:6: "And let him who is instructed in the Word share in all that is good with him who is instructing." This would be fine, if they were teaching obedience to Yahuah's Torah and held to the belief in Yahusha. They are lawless, rejecting the instructions for living as given by Yahuah. They abhor **obedience**.

They are masters at twisting Scriptures, and therefore they are "**blind guides.**" They teach their own traditions; the commandments of men.

Their rules and traditions are not to be questioned, yet they claim Yahuah's Torah is *"too difficult,"* and *"no one is able to keep His Torah."* Yahuah said it is **<u>not</u>** too difficult.

"For this command which I am commanding you today, it is not too hard for you, nor is it far off." (Dt. 30:11)

In the context of this verse we find the curses for **disobedience** to His Torah:

We would not remain in the land, but be driven into the nations until we perish.

Yahuah has never taught anyone to do anything that is toxic (poison) for them.

Yahuah's Torah is behavioral training in how to **love**.

Babel is the "woman" we're **called-out** from, and she is religion.

Her traditions have molded the minds of nations for thousands of years. Tradition is the gravity that imprisons hearts, keeping them from receiving

Yahuah's Word, and His Name. His **Name** and His **Word** are above all (Psalm 138:2), so the dragon and the false prophet attack these two things above all. The **Word** and the **Name** are attacked constantly.

Yahusha searches for those with whom He can have companionship. His Spirit is repelled by religion, which blinds us with **men's traditions**.
Every week, millions listen to teachings that inoculate them against returning to the everlasting Covenant of kindness. They are taught the Commandments have been "done away", and a "New Covenant" of "only believe" is now in place. They are programmed to believe Yahuah's Torah is "impossible for anyone to keep." Some have said the Commandments were given to man to prove they could not by obeyed.

The dragon continually fights against the Truth. The Covenant is considered toxic, **poison** to the minds of children. To escape the lawlessness, we have to decide whom we will serve; Yahuah, or men's teachings (see Rom 6:16). The whole western world is under the influence of the culture that hatched at Alexandria.

The church / circus fathers and headmasters allegorized Scripture, and slowly molded a powerful hierarchy over all the illiterate masses. Rome enforced the idea the church had *superseded* and *replaced* the people of Yisharal, who they taught had been rejected by "Kurios" (the LORD). They invented sacraments, and Christograms to encode the Name of Yahusha (IC-XC, HIS, IESV), eventually changing it to Jesus.

HERE IS THE TORAH TO GUARD:
"**Remember the Torah of Mosheh**, My servant, which I commanded him in Horeb for all Yisharal – laws and right-rulings. See, I am sending you AliYahu the prophet before the coming of the great and awesome Day of Yahuah. And he shall turn the hearts of the fathers to the children, and the hearts of the children to their fathers, lest I come and smite the Earth with **utter destruction**."
(Malaki 4:4-6)

Yahusha told us to pray that our flight not be in winter, or on the **Shabath** at Mt. 24:20. Shabath is the sign between Yahuah and His people forever.

From the pattern we see in this world, it appears the followers of the dragon have chosen Malaki 4's smiting of the Earth with utter destruction. They are decidedly against the **Torah of Mosheh.**

RULERS OF EVIL

Link to YouTube video:
https://youtu.be/XeKnxfTkKm4
Rulers Of Evil
Who benefits from war? Follow the money.

It flows to the machinery produced by the military industrial complex. Today the medical industry has been weaponized also.

You may have never heard about the REGIMINI MILITANTIS UNIVERSAE, but it has been using financial leverage to engulf the world's leaders in great chaos. When a plane crashed with hundreds of passengers many years ago, the report also mentioned that the purchasing officer for the USAF was one of the casualties. JFK Jr. died in a crash just as his political aspirations were developing. These and many other suspicious events go on all the time.

Conspiratorial & Accidental views matter when compared side-by-side. The Truth surrounding the JFK assassination, the first executive action taken by Johnson, and the real crisis of Vietnam is now obvious, but the media is digging itself into a bigger hole because its involvement is real.

Eisenhower warned us about the rise of the Military Industrial Complex in his farewell speech in 1961:

"Until the latest of our world conflicts, the United States had no armaments industry. American makers of plowshares could, with time and as required, make swords as well. But we can no longer risk emergency improvisation of national defense. We have been compelled to create a permanent armaments industry of vast proportions. Added to this, 3.5 million men & women are directly engaged in the defense establishment.

We annually spend on military security alone more than the net income of all United States corporations.

This conjunction of an immense military establishment and a large arms industry is new in the American experience.

The total influence—economic, political, even spiritual—is felt in every city, every Statehouse, every office of the Federal government.

We recognize the imperative need for this development. Yet, we must not fail to comprehend its grave implications.

Our toil, resources, and livelihood are all involved. So is the very structure of our society.

In the councils of government, we must guard against the acquisition of unwarranted influence, whether sought or unsought, by the military-industrial complex.

The potential for the disastrous rise of misplaced power exists and will persist. We must never let the weight of this combination endanger our liberties or democratic processes. We should take nothing for granted. Only an alert and knowledgeable citizenry can compel the proper meshing of the huge industrial and military machinery of defense with our peaceful methods and goals, so that security and liberty may prosper together."

Dwight D. Eisenhower, farewell speech excerpt (1961)

We need to examine the crisis that sparked the Vietnam conflict, and how two world powers took advantage and perpetuated it for as long as possible. Hundreds of thousands died directly, and nearly 40,000 more from unexploded munitions well after the war ended. I lived through this, but many young men I knew did not. Landmines are still killing innocent children in deserts.

Christians killing Christians is accomplished by politically socializing the young to fight for "their country." Yahusha will judge those responsible. By the time JFK became the US president, the Vietnam conflict was in full swing, and *he intended to end US support. He didn't live long after that.*

It was a war against Buddhists, and the persecutor was the Roman Catholic leader of South Vietnam. Two world powers supplied the armaments, and many young men gave their lives to enrich the manufacturers of those armaments. Yahuah's vengeance does not sleep.

To attract the attention of world media to the Catholic persecution of his Buddhist brothers, a Vietnamese Mahayana monk burned himself to death at a busy Saigon intersection, 6-11-1963. His name was *Thich Quang Duc.*

The South Vietnamese president Diem, a staunch Roman Catholic, was backed by the US under the guise of "communist infiltrators."

These are a few things that must be connected, but few see it:

June 11, 1963:

Self immolation of Buddhist monk Thich Quang Duc in Saigon sparks outrage around the world and brings attention to conflict.

July 2, 1963:

JFK meets with Regimini Militantis Universae at Rome.

Nov. 1-2, 1963:

President Diem and his brother Ngo Dinh Nhu are murdered during a coup by dissident generals of the South Vietnamese army.

Nov. 22, 1963:

JFK assassinated and Johnson is sworn-in as president. While still in flight after being sworn-in as US President, Johnson revoked JFK's executive order to end US support in Vietnam.

Aug. 2-4, 1964:

Two supposed incidents in the Gulf of Tonkin lead Johnson to seek congressional approval for direct U.S. involvement.

The average age of the "enemy" at this point was 12 years old.

The Unseen Hand, An Introduction To the Conspiratorial View of History by Ralph Epperson is a book that you may want to add to your library. Ralph compares the *accidental view* of history with what he calls the *conspiratorial view.* By far, most major events are being directed everywhere all the time, and the media spins them for public consumption.

After generations of living with men's teaching authorities, the whole world is spiraling down morally, and spinning out of control. They have turned their ears away from listening to Yahuah's Torah, His Covenant of love. If we abide in Yahusha and obey His Word, we are truly His taught ones, and we will know the Truth, and the Truth will set us free (Yn. 8).

The truth of why JFK was killed and another came behind him to do the will of the arms manufacturers is obvious.

The media is a useful idiot that serves another agenda. They keep the JFK mystery going.

In several of my books there is an admission that I was taught by the best educators this planet has ever known, the **Jesuits** (aka, Jesuit Illuminati). They educate the children of upwardly-mobile politicians and businessmen to prepare them for future leaders within the clergy, or as operatives within governments and industry when they are older.

These schools are openly called "prep-schools." This order was founded by Inigo Loyola (a Spanish soldier turned priest) in 1534 with the prime directive of restoring

authoritarian papal power. The papacy had lost its power as a result of the nobles turning away during the **Reformation.**

The Societas IESV was established as a **militant** order, the Counter-Reformation, to use any and all means necessary, even assassination, to bring governments under their influence. The *Jesuit general* is the real head of the Roman Circus. Regimini militantis Ecclesiae was the papal bull promulgated by Pope Paul III September 27, 1540, giving first approval to the Society of Jesus.

It is a military order, nothing more.

Look up the **Jesuit Oath of Induction** if you are interested in how far they will go to achieve their goals. Their prime objective is to assure their control over the people.

Jesuits knew that the path to restoring power was through the **children** of the Nobility, so they became educators. Ignatius Loyola founded the Jesuit order, and quoted Aristotle with the words,

"Give me a child until he is seven, and I will show you the man."

This *psychotherapy* holds a billion people under its influence, and it took Yahusha to snap me out of it. Do you want to awaken others from their delusion?

Does A Day Really Begin At Midnight?
NekemYah (Nehemiah) 13:19 is one of many witnesses to when the 7th day of rest begins:
"And it came to be, at the gates of Yerushalim, as it began to be dark before the Shabath, that I commanded the gates to be shut, and commanded that they should not be opened till after the Shabath. And I stationed some of my servants at the gates, so that no burdens would be brought in on the Shabath day."
The day of rest is evening-to-evening. It would make no sense to shut the gates of Yerushalim before dawn, but some struggle to make it appear so for their doctrinal perspective to work. Cognitive dissonance is stress caused by faulty reasoning, but Natsarim are here to point out the inconsistencies.
http://www.fossilizedcustoms.com/day.html

Natsarim Are Different From Christians
Natsarim teach obedience. Romans 6:16 tells us we are the servants of the one we obey. We use the real Hebrew Name of our Deliverer: YAHUSHA. Yahusha ordered the first Natsarim to teach all nations His Name, and to obey everything He commanded. He warned us that we would encounter great resistance, and far worse.
The traditions of men are highly thought of, but are abominations, and to be purged from our minds. That which is highly thought of among men is an abomination in the sight of Alahim (Luke 16:14-15).

Adding and taking away from the Word by men's guidance has led the whole world into confusion (Isaiah / YashaYahu 9:16).
They are the leaven Yahusha spoke of as men's teachings (Luke 12, Mark 8).
On Shabath (7th day of each week), we stop and rest in our dwellings, do no servile work or buying and selling, from sunset to sunset. Shemoth / Exodus 16 will show this. We are resting, and remember that Yahuah rested, and set the 7th day apart. No traveling or commerce is allowed.
The old covenant involving animal blood for atonement is obsolete (Hebrews 8:13, Dt. 31:26). We do not follow 613 commandments, or the Talmud. Any animals we eat are clean. We observe the appointed times at Dt. 16, and guard the Ten Commandments at Dt. 5.
The Truth sets us free from the traditions added by men (John / Yahukanon 8:31-32).
"I am the Vine, you are the Natsarim."
(John / Yahukanon 15:5).
We know who we are because we know Who Yahusha is. We are the servant of the one we obey (see Romans 6:16).

Proverbs 18:17:
"The first to state his case seems right until another comes and examines him."
The Jesuits programmed the world to believe that JESUS is the one name of the Deliverer, and seared their consciences by showing a dead body on a symbol of the Sun for them to bow down to.
The Truth is: The one Name (Acts 4:12) of the Deliverer is YAHUSHA, a Name in Hebrew meaning "I am your Deliverer," and He is raising up His

Natsarim (Acts 24:5) to cry out (YirmeYahu / Jeremiah 31:6) here in the endtimes?
Remember: 2 Timothy 3:16 – All Scripture matters.

The Truth Has Fallen In The Streets
Our redemption from the penalty of violating the Commandments is solely by the blood of Yahusha, the Lamb of Alahim.
He ended the animal blood offerings and old priesthood, and our trust in His death and resurrection is the only permanent solution offered to mankind. If a person willfully turns back to being a criminal by violating the Commandments after receiving the empowering Spirit of Yahusha to become His servant, and will not repent of living in such a state of rebellion, Hebrews 10 explains what their outcome will be. 1 Yahukanon / John 2:4 helps us understand why: they don't know Yahusha, but claim they do.
Belief comes by hearing. Natsarim teach the true Name of our Redeemer, and guard the Name and the Word; the dragon is enraged about this Commandment-keeping (Rev. 12:17). We know the way of Truth has been maligned (2 Peter 2:2). People think lawlessness is acceptable as long as they do and believe what their pastors tell them. The pagan practices are fixed in their minds, keeping the simple comfortable with familiar traditions. By studying the Scriptures, we get the Truth, and the Truth sets us free from the leaven of men.

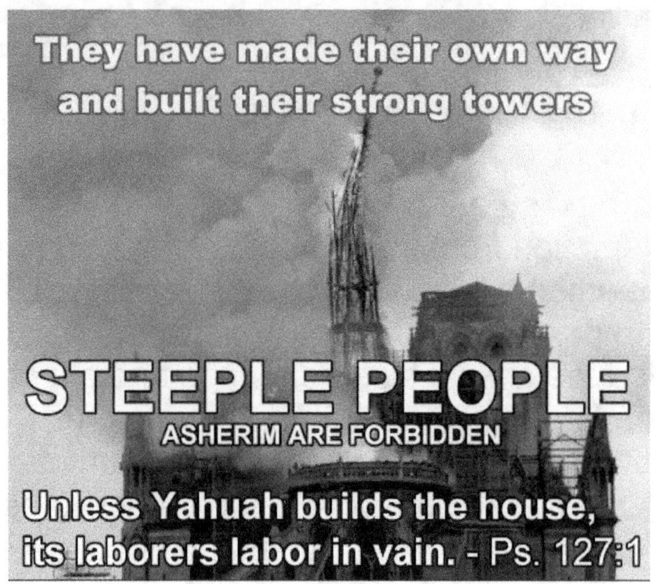

The builders of the Magisterium are the NIKOLAITANS

Definition from reference.com on-line encyclopedia: **"The meaning of the name, *'victors over the people'* or *'rulers over the world'* suggests to some of these authors that the Nikolaitans were among those who maintained that there must be a <u>religious</u> <u>hierarchy</u> to control the spiritual development of the common people; it is believed they were trying to set themselves up as priests in a <u>two-class</u> system – one that would give them absolute control over the laity (common people), who would be completely dependent upon them for all spiritual knowledge, guidance, and access to (Yahuah)."** Important point: The primary stronghold of the Nikolaitans and those who allow them to persist: *Believing they know the path of salvation.*

The **two-class system**, priests over people, is seen

44

by many to be the core reason for the undoing of the original assemblies of **Natsarim.*** Men seek to be recognized or distinguished from the ordinary folk, and often dress the part. Appearances are most important to them, and their behavior is an act to be seen by men. Hypocrisy and eye-service is condemned by Yahusha, as we shall see in this study. They are playing a role, and expect that everyone should acknowledge their authority and status. They seek after titles and honors.
These verses escape their attention:

Mat 23:8 ***"But you, do not be called 'Rabbi,' for One is your Teacher, the Mashiak, and you are all brothers."***
Yahusha summed-up by saying this at Mt. 23:12:
"And whoever exalts himself shall be humbled, and whoever humbles himself shall be exalted."
A ***stronghold*** is a false belief or notion.

Strongholds can be broken by simply *knowing* they are there.
2Korinthians 10-6:
"For the weapons we fight with are not fleshly but mighty in Alahim for overthrowing <u>strongholds</u>, overthrowing reasonings and every high matter that exalts itself against the knowledge of Alahim, taking captive every thought to make it obedient to the Mashiak, and being ready to punish all disobedience, when your obedience is complete."

"So you also have those who adhere to the teaching of the Nikolaitans, which teaching I hate." - Rev. 2

At Acts 20, Paul called a meeting of all elders and warned them: ***"For I know this, that after my departure savage wolves shall come in among you, not sparing the flock. Also from among yourselves men shall arise, speaking distorted teachings, to draw away the taught ones <u>after themselves</u>."***

*The following is a list of those who held their leadership positions in 2011. The **people** change over time, but the purpose here is to illustrate how groups have held authority over the diverse masses who look to them for guidance.*

Supreme Judaism leader: *14 Million Followers: Rabbi Yona Metzger, Chief Rabbi of Israel, teaches Talmud of Akiba + TaNaK.*
Judaism is essentially the modern form of the Pharisees, built upon the teachings of Akiba.
All Pharisees were known by the title rabbi; the term is not found in the TaNaK. It means "my exalted one" or "my master."

Islamic Imams: *1.6 Billion Followers*
Sunni and Shia sects are rivals, in perpetual conflict. Abdul Alim Musa states that the United States will be "the Islamic State of North America" by 2050 CE.

Note: the use of prayer beads came before Islam from the worship of Shiva. The Shiva shrines, stone, circumambulating, etc., came from India by way of the Silk Road, reaching the Middle East about 200 BCE.

Supreme Sikh leader: *23 Million Followers*
Giani Joginder Singh Vedanti, India
No hair cutting - a blend of Hinduism and Islam.

Supreme Lutheran leader: *65 Million Followers*
*Mark S. Hanson; this group dispenses three
sacraments, believe in a trinity; remains very, very
Catholic in many ways, leaving behind the
indulgences and papal authority. They still obey the
pope and Constantine because they believe that
Sun-day is the Sabbath. Catholicism is defined as
the belief in "one god in three persons."*
*This definition is according to the Creed of
Athanasius.*
*They promote the idea of LENT, a practice from
Babel involving 40 days of fasting / weeping over
the death of Tammuz.*

A reminder again of the important point: The primary
stronghold of the Nikolaitans and those who allow
them to persist by supporting them:
Believing they know the path of salvation.

Supreme Buddhist leader: *376 Million Followers*
Tenzin Gyatoso,
*14th Dalai Lama of Tibet (A derivative of Hinduism)
Karma, reincarnation, Samsara, Nirvana, no deities,
only a* **life force**
*objective: achieve nothingness, oblivion, by way of
dharma, the way of enlightenment.*
Humanists love this man.

Buddhist prayer beads are the source of the Islamic prayer beads, an ancient form of repetitive prayers similar to the practice of circumambulating or walking around an object of worship.
The beads derive from the Hindu deity Shiva, and represent Shiva's tears.
See book, **Who Is Allah, The Hindu Connection**

Supreme Hindu leader: *900 Million Followers*
"Amma" Sri Mata Amritanandamayi in Amritapuri, India
hundreds of deities, Samsara
Practices sorcery for healing and divination

Supreme Anglican Catholic: *73 Million Followers*
Rowan Williams, Archbishop of Canterbury, London
Same as Roman Catholic, except they deny authority of papacy
This circus follows Sunday, Easter, and all of Constantine's precepts. They do not live by every Word that proceeds from the mouth of Yahuah.

Supreme Eastern Orthodox: *240 Million Followers*
led by His Holiness Aleksi II, Patriarch of Moscow
Same program of salvation as Rome: **sacraments**

Supreme Roman Catholic Magisterium:
Over 1 Billion Followers, "His Holiness" and "Holy Father" are titles usurped from Yahuah Himself, whom the holder of this office considers himself!

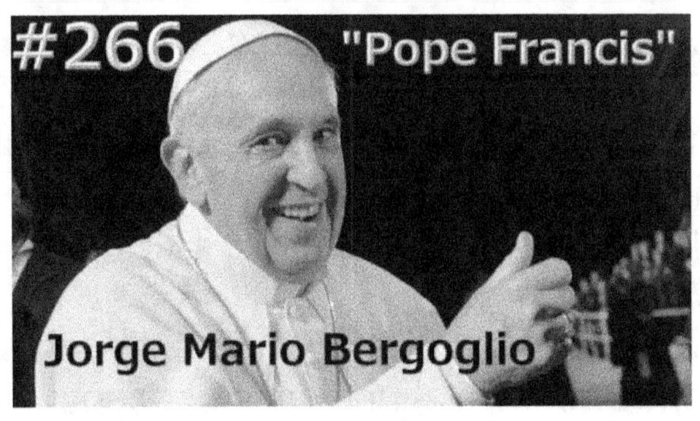

He's the vicar of Nimrod, but uses the title Vicar of Christ. **RCC TEACHING:**

ETERNAL LIFE IS MERITED BY RECEIVING GRACE FROM SACRAMENTS DISPENSED THROUGH PRIESTS

THEY CHANGED THE 10 COMMANDMENTS, AND HAVE IDOLS, EAT PORK, AND THINK DIES SOLIS (SUN-DAY) IS THE SABBATH NOW, BUT OUTLAWED THE TRUE SHABATH OF YAHUAH IN 365-370 AT THE COUNCIL OF LAODICEA

THE PRAYER-BEAD THING, AGAIN?

Latin, rosarium, or crown of roses
THE RCC ADOPTED THIS PAGAN PRACTICE IN THE YEAR 1090 CE, FROM THE HINDU SHIVA-WORSHIPING ARABS. THE ARABS EMBRACED MANY HINDU PRACTICES INTO THEIR ISLAMIC CUSTOMS
Praying to the dead is divination, but this practice comes from Babel via Hinduism's concepts of ancestor worship.
Reincarnation and necromancy, holy water, Purgatory, indulgences, and Shiva beads all downloaded into Catholicism about the same time.

Ex-prime minister of UK, Tony Blair, converted from Anglican Catholic Church to Roman Catholic, December 2007
Seeks salvation through 7 Sacraments (and rosary prayers) dispensed through Catholic priesthood's magisterium

SCIENTOLOGY:
*A **galactic boss** is waited for by the 22 million followers of Xenu, **the galactic boss.***
L. Ron Hubbard - founded his church in 1954.
*Born 1911, Nebraska. Hubbard discovered he could make more money in religion than in writing science fiction, so he designed a new set of beliefs (religion) called **Dianetics**.*
Dianetics solves "engrams" (traumas) stored in the soul (theta).
Objective: To erase the engrams to a state of "clear" through the help of spiritual auditors and an electronic gizmo (E-meter).
Some of the teachings include this historical gem:
"75 million years ago, there was an alien

galactic ruler named Xenu who was in charge of 76 planets in our sector of the galaxy, including planet Earth."
According to Scientology, our problems are caused by the spirits of **space aliens inhabiting our bodies**.
Tom Cruise converted to this belief (1990).

Thomas Cruise Mapother, aka, Tom Cruise, born 1962.
Tom attended the Jesuit St. Xavier High School in Louisville, KY, and desired to become a priest at age 14.
This author was indoctrinated at this <u>same</u> Jesuit school for 4 years, just 12 years before Tom attended.
In 1990 Tom renounced his devout Catholic beliefs after he embraced The Church Of Scientology, claiming that the Scientology teachings had cured him of the dyslexia that had plagued him all of his life. He had belief based on *signs and wonders.* (See Mt. 12:39). May Yahusha call him to the Truth one day soon.

Rom 16:17,18: ***"Now I call upon you, brothers, watch out for those who cause divisions and stumbling, contrary to the teaching*** (instruction, TORAH) ***which you learned, and turn away from them. For such ones do not serve our Master Yahusha Mashiak, but their own stomach, and by smooth words and flattering speech they deceive the hearts of the innocent."***
False teachings hold people captive in strongholds.

Making a *name* for their division and the **teachings**

they adhere to is what is known as a *denomination* today. These divisions are defined by their individual names, and the doctrinal society (strongholds) they associate with. None of these divisions are endorsed by the Writings of Truth.

DIVISIONS ARE NOT OF YAHUAH, THEY ARE A SCHEME OF THE DEVIL - THESE DIVISIONS FOLLOW THE EARLY TEACHINGS OF THE CATECHETICAL SCHOOL OF ALEXANDRIA, PAGAN PRACTICES FROM THE ANCIENT WORLD

Men often **name** their ministries after *themselves,* but the only true foundation is Yahusha.
1Korinthians 1:10-13 ***"And I appeal to you brothers, by the Name of our Master Yahusha Mashiak, that you all agree, and that there be <u>no divisions</u> among you, but that you be knit together in the same mind and in the same opinion.***
For I have been informed concerning you, my brothers, by those of the house of Kloe, that there are strifes (quarrels, variances, debates) ***among you.***
What I mean is this, that each one of you says, 'I am of Paul,' or 'I am of Apollos,' or 'I am of Kefa,' or 'I am of Mashiak'.
Has the Mashiak been divided? Was Paul impaled for you?
Or were you immersed in the name of Paul?"

We are to be <u>one</u> body, without divisions, and no E-meters, sacraments, holy water, or galactic bosses are needed.
Nikolaitans are not our intercessors. Wherever two or more are gathered, Yahusha is there with us. In every time and place, Yahusha is accessible to us

all.
Mat 18:20: *"For where two or three are gathered together in My Name, there I am in their midst."*
The Oral Law, or Talmud, requires a quorum of 10 men (called a minyan). Talmud is considered to be the codification of halakah, but Yahusha **invalidated** this idea. The **teachings of the fathers** was a heavy **yoke** (body of teachings), but our only teaching authority is Yahusha.

Division is the challenge, and love is the answer. This is why the humble will inherit the reign of Yahuah: they put others before themselves.

A reminder again of the important point: The primary stronghold of the Nikolaitans and those who allow them to persist by supporting them:
Believing they know the path of salvation.

Mar 9:33-35: **"And they came to Kafar Nakum, and having come in the house He asked them, 'What was it you disputed among yourselves on the way?' And they were silent, for on the way they had disputed with one another *who was the greatest*. And sitting down, He called the twelve and said to them, *'If anyone wishes to be first, he shall be last of all and servant of all.'"***

Jeremiah / YirmeYahu 9:24:
"'but let him who boasts boast of this, that he understands and knows Me, that I am Yahuah, doing kindness, right-ruling, and righteousness in the earth. For in these I delight,' declares Yahuah."

Alternative to men's traditions: The Word
Which Yoke, Yahusha's or Man's?
There is still a division over what some perceive as
traditions "orally" handed-down.
Every Word of Yahuah was written, and read aloud
to the people. The oral instructions, or traditions of
the fathers, was the paradigm Paul said was his
former way of living by. He called it "Yahudaism."
"For you have heard of my former way of life in
Yahudaism, how intensely I persecuted the
assembly of Alahim, and ravaged it." - Gal 1:13.
Note the phrase, "former way of life."
This "yoke" (teaching authority) of men is what is
being described here also:
"Now then, why do you try Alahim by putting a yoke
on the neck of the taught ones which neither our
fathers nor we were able to bear?" - Acts 15:10.
It is what was added (the leaven of men's
teachings) that Yahusha called "old wine."
The traditions of men are the object-lesson from
Matsah (Unleavened Bread). We must become
unleavened, purging the teaching authorities and
corrupting influences of men's ideas. Men's
teachings block the pure and clean objective of
love, which the Torah's goal is to teach us.
https://www.torahzone.net/Beware-the-Blob-
Free-pdf-Download.html

**What will happen to people who listen to false
teachings?**
Romans 10:14 helps to explain how important our
mission is, and that someone has to be sent, then
speak to the lost. The blame for never hearing the
Truth is not on the ones who never hear it, but it
falls on *the deceiver* who altered and diverted

everything toward Sun worship (that is, the king of Babel, *the dragon*). His servants are masquerading as messengers of light (2 Korinthians 11:13-15). YashaYahu 14 describes this fallen being, and his end. Yahusha is the only Judge, and we must test all things to see if they align with His Word. If we reject Truth, we will be sent a strong delusion (2 Thessalonians 2:11), and our chains will be tightened for as long as we continue mocking and believing lies (YashaYahu 28:22).

WORMWOOD

Changing the Word of Yahuah causes wormwood. Wormwood is a bitterness toward the idea of obedience. Try to imagine Yahusha teaching people to alter the day He rested on each week while living among men. Now imagine Him punishing those who obey His Commandments, and rewarding those who follow men's traditions.
Wormwood is literally everywhere.
Link to video: https://youtu.be/tGgcJ6wS9gw
The teachings of men have changed the Torah, and violated the Everlasting Covenant.

Release Is Coming

Yahusha told us to watch for His return.
The days prior to His return will rapidly turn into a living nightmare for the inhabitants of the Earth. The events unleashed will terrify most, yet a few of us will lift-up our heads because we see our Redeemer, Who loves us, approaching. I can't say that any perception we might form in our minds of the timing of Yahusha's return will prepare anyone, but there has to be an important connection to the

10th day of the 7th month (Lev. 25:9-10), and how it relates to His **redemption plan**.

The main idea that we should remember about the days being shortened for the sake of the chosen ones is to give us *hope*, and not *despair* in the midst of the wrath poured-out *around us*. Yahusha wants us to be assured that He knows who He has sealed for the day that is coming, and to trust in Him, not our own understanding. He knows those who are His. His thoughts for us are always good, and He has wonderful plans for us. Watch a video on this: https://youtu.be/Wcz-qtY4_J8
Our inheritance is about to be restored to us, and His Name is Yahusha.

On the day Yahuah pours out His fiery wrath on the disobedient inhabitants, His chosen ones will be among the people being burned, but it will not harm them. Those who have been immersed and called on the Name of Yahusha will be delivered on the day of the redemption of our bodies, but false ideas about getting "raptured" have misled many people. Yahusha described it in His parable of the wheat and tares, **"First, gather the weeds to be burned; then gather the wheat into My barn."**
Psalm 91 describes this event, and because we know His Name, He will deliver us.

The Dead Sea Scrolls Under Siege
The latest attempt to deflect attention from the DSS is to cast doubt on their provenance, and make them appear to be forgeries in the mind of the public.
The DSS is the greatest archaeological find in human history. The Word of Yahuah is infinitely

more valuable than any treasure such as gold and silver stored in the tombs of dead Farahs (Greek, Pharaohs).

Mt. 23:24: ***"You blind guides! You strain out a gnat, but swallow a camel."***

Those behind the cover-up of the Name of Yahuah have reached a point of desperation.
The papal bull in 2008 only brought more attention to the Tetragrammaton, not less.
From 1947 to the present, the Jesuit scroll team has worked tirelessly to divert attention away from the DSS. The real reason the scrolls were there in the first place was because the Name of Yahuah is written on the artifacts, and that is the camel the Jesuits never wanted the world to know about.
There are no gnats (niqqud marks) on any of the artifacts in the the 11 original caves at Kumeran (Qumran).
The scrolls are the real thing, and not forgeries.
http://www.fossilizedcustoms.com/deadseascrolls.html

If Christians began to live like Yahusha lived, they would cease to be Christians. They would be obedient to Yahusha's Commandments, and abandon their former way of life following traditions. They would not go to steeples in the morning on the first day of each week, and they would know Leviticus 26:1 prohibits building them.

Easter: The modern term for the Norse fertility deity of the dawn Eostre, the Egyptian Isis, the Roman Uenus, the Greek Aphrodite, the Hindu Gauri, and

Ishtar, Babel's mother of harlots. Easter popped into the Anglican Catholic KJV at Acts 12:4 in 1611, but is not in any other translation before or since.
http://www.fossilizedcustoms.com/easter.html

When did LENT start happening to us?
LENT - An observance adopted by Catholic Christianity from a former practice from Babel involving *ashes* and *fasting*. The women *"weeping for Tammuz"* are mentioned at Ezekiel 8:14.
This video will connect the dots for you to decide whether it is pleasing to our Creator Yahuah, or not.
Watch the youtube video:
https://youtu.be/snO7VIWmrLw
Ash Wednesday to Ishtar Sun Day is their span of 40 days, and billions are unfamiliar with how it became mixed into the practices they observe.

Did Yahuah tell us it's OK to adopt pagan customs if we practice them with new intentions, and even divert them toward serving Him?
Let's search the Writing of Truth and see:

"These are the laws and directives which you guard to do in the land which Yahuah Alahim of

your fathers is giving you to possess, all the Yomim that you live on the soil. Completely destroy all the places where the guyim which you are dispossessing served their mighty ones, on the high mountains and on the hills and under every green tree. And you shall break down their altars, and smash their pillars, and burn their asherim (*trees*) with fire. And you shall cut down the carved images of their mighty ones and shall destroy their name out of that place. Do not do so to Yahuah your Alahim, but seek the place which Yahuah your Alahim chooses, out of all your tribes, to put His Name there, for His Mishkan, and there you shall enter." Dt. 12:1-5

In a second place we read this:
"Guard, and obey all these words which I command you, that it might be well with you and your children after you forever, when you do what is good and right in the eyes of Yahuah your Alahim. When Yahuah your Alahim does cut off from before you the guyim which you go to dispossess, and you dispossess them and dwell in their land, guard yourself that you are not ensnared to follow them, after they are destroyed from before you, and that you do not inquire about their mighty ones, saying, 'How did these guyim serve their mighty ones? And let me do so too.' Do not do so to Yahuah your Alahim, for every abomination which Yahuah hates they have done to their mighty ones, for they even burn their sons and daughters in the fire to their mighty ones. All the words I am

**commanding you, guard to do it – do not add to
it nor take away from it.**" – Dt. 12:28-32

Do You Believe In Grace?
Kasid (commonly seen spelled chasid or hesed)
means *kindness*, and the word is found throughout
the Writing of Truth. Often it is translated with the
word mercy. Yahuah's kindness is everlasting. An
interlinear Hebrew-English example of the word can
be seen at verse 17 of Psalm 103.
Yahuah's kindness toward sinners who repent and
turn back to His eternal Covenant shows His
kindness is everlasting, and give hope for all
mankind. Yahusha came to deliver us from the
penalty of death through His blood, ending the old
covenant using the temporary covering through
animal blood.
Repenting of our sinfulness first, we then call on
Yahusha's Name and beg His forgiveness for our
sins at our immersion in water. This seals us with
His Name for the day of the redemption of our
bodies, and His indwelling gives us His Mind in
order to know what is pleasing to Him. To know Him
is to obey His Commandments, thus overcoming
the works of the devil. We no longer continue to live
in our old mind of the flesh, nor thinking our
rebellion and ignorance can continue unabated.
To sin willfully after receiving a knowledge of the
Truth carries a heavy penalty, which may be read
about in verses 26 & 27 of Hebrews chapter 10.

Come Out Of Babel
YashaYahu 48:16-20:
*"Come near to Me, hear this: I have not spoken
in secret from the beginning; from the time that*

it was, I was there. And now Aduni Yahuah has sent Me, and His Ruach." Thus said Yahuah, your Redeemer, the Qodesh One of Yisharal, 'I am Yahuah your Alahim, teaching you what is best, leading you by the way you should go. If only you had listened to My commands! Then your peace would have been like a river, and your obedience like the waves of the sea. And your seed would have been like the sand, and the offspring of your inward parts like the grains of sand. His name would not have been cut off nor destroyed from before Me. Come out of Babel! Flee from the Kaldeans! Declare this with a voice of singing, proclaim it, send it out to the end of the arets! Say, 'Yahuah has redeemed His servant Yaqub!'"

Watch a video shared on two youtube channels at the links below that reveals how far we have fallen from FAVOR.

Can we be restored to FAVOR while we continue to transgress the eternal Covenant?

What Is Grace?

Favor and kindness are the Hebrew meaning of KASID, but Christianity sprouted among pagans who worshiped ZEUS. Traditions handed-down many errors in the words the world has embraced, and now it's time to awaken to Truth, and learn what is pleasing to Yahusha.

The Graces were three daughters of Zeus, and a Charis (as in Charismatic) refers to one of these. Our mouths are polluted with pagan terms; now it's time to come out of Babel. Youtube link to short video:

https://youtu.be/kuOVxrmuPAM

Unconditional love?
Can we ignore the eternal Covenant of love and live as if Sinai never happened?
Does Yahusha love us without any conditions?
Or rather, will the sinner who repents have all his sins wiped away.
If we return to the former life of sin, can we expect the mythical "unconditional love" gospel to comfort us on the day we stand before Yahusha?
https://youtu.be/HQ4WiaB1t9o

Our teachers are leading us astray by lying to us. The one we obey is who we serve.

Faith, Belief, And The Ideas Behind Them
People hear the over-used word *faith* so often from teachers and Scripture translations the word becomes nebulous and non-specific.
Belief without obedience is a useless belief.
Teachers who talk about *unconditional love* and *faith* are also disengaged from Torah, and very engaged with traditions. Everyone we teach should become teachers and become like their teachers.
If we use words to instill *obedience*, rather than only *thought-oriented concepts* (like faith), our hearers will not be triggered by what preachers have put into their minds. The Word goes forth from the mouth of Yahuah to perform the purpose for which it was sent into the world.*
Let's be doers of the Word; not hearers only. Show your belief by what you practice, and give your belief legs - make it happen, and obvious to everyone. Don't hide your light; put it right out there in the open so others may WALK in it.

ACCEPTANCE PLEDGE

1
YOU ARE YAHUAH OUR ALAHIM
NO OTHER IS BEFORE YOUR FACE

2
WE BOW TO NO IMAGES

3
WE DO NOT CAST THE NAME OF
YAHUAH OUR ALAHIM TO RUIN

4
WE REMEMBER SHABATH
TO GUARD IT AS QODESH

5
WE RESPECT OUR FATHER & MOTHER

6
WE DO NOT MURDER

7
WE DO NOT BREAK WEDLOCK

8
WE DO NOT STEAL

9
WE DO NOT BEAR A MALICIOUS
WITNESS AGAINST OUR NEIGHBOR

10
WE DO NOT COVET OUR NEIGHBOR'S
WIFE, HOUSE, FIELD, SERVANTS,
ANIMALS, OR OTHER POSSESSIONS
OF OUR NEIGHBOR

PLEDGED TO YAHUSHA WHO LOVES US
AND HAS FREED US BY HIS BLOOD

I AM YAHUAH, THAT IS MY NAME
LOVE ME AND GUARD MY COMMANDS
LOVE YOUR NEIGHBOR AS YOURSELF
LOVE ONE ANOTHER AS I HAVE LOVED YOU

TORAHZONE.NET   LAMBLEGACYFOUNDATION.COM   NATSARIMSEARCH.COM

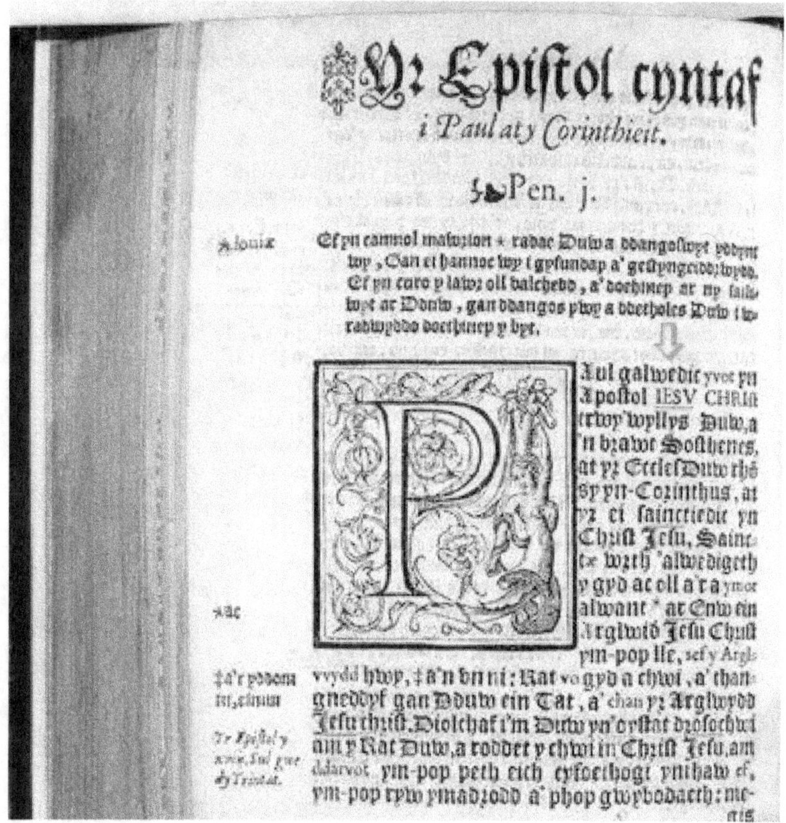

Who Is <u>IESV</u>?

Although the Anglican Circus (Kirche) is still referred to as *Anglican Catholic*, most Protestants don't realize they too embrace many dogmas which originated in the Great Mother Circus.

The first edition of the KJV shows the underlined <u>IESV</u> christogram replacing the Name of Yahusha, take directly from the Latin Vulgate. There is only one Name - Acts 4:12 - but it was altered by translators. King James (Yaqub in Eberith) was baptized as a baby in a Catholic ceremony. Sunday (Ravivara in Hindu), trinitarianism (Hindu), solar symbols (Suns, cruxes), pagan costumes, indoor altars, and many other patterns inherited from our fathers are addressed at YirmeYahu (Jer.) 16:19 & Danial 12.

Pearl Of Great Price

The seeker of Truth must dig for the true Hebrew Name of the Creator, and by-pass the Greco-Roman culture taught by the Alexandrian circus fathers. There is great pressure against the Name. The papal bull of 2008 forbids the utterance of it in public. Demons love the name JESUS, and that is because it is only a name invented very recently. The letter J is less than 500 years old, and was not even in the first edition of the Anglican-Katholic translation known as the KJV. The IESV (with bar, or titlos) is shown in a photo of that edition, standing in place of the true Name, Yahusha. This IESV is a christogram, and came straight from the Katholic version known as the Latin Vulgate.

Language Confusion

There's a false association between YAH (YOD-HAY) and the Egyptian moon deity Aah.

The phonetic association is purely based on how the words SOUND to the ears of those doing research without a thorough knowledge of the Truth of Scripture and proper archaeological study.
http://www.fossilizedcustoms.com/lexomorphosis.html

The Name We Call On Matters
When **AliYahu** (aka Elijah) demonstrated the importance of the Name, he asked the people why they wavered between two opinions (1 Kings 18). As much as it depends on us, we have to spread the most accurate Truth possible. Indistinct utterances, repeating words we don't understand, and having no desire to learn more about His Name shows a level of exposure to the intoxicating effects of the weed seed (meaning that it looks like Truth, but it's really the darnel). Paul taught about languages (tongues, speaking intelligibly) and the importance of interpretation, otherwise the hearer perceives the speaker to be a barbarian.
Even lifeless musical instruments have to sound the melody clearly, he explains, or the hearers will not recognize the tune being played (1 Korinthians 14). At Romans 10, Paul asks how can they call on the Name unless someone is sent to speak it to them. The Name of Yahuah is four vowels, and as our Deliverer we call on Him in the Name Yahusha, meaning "I am your Deliverer."

GOT OIL?
Substitutions For YAHUAH:
LORD, Dominus, Kyrios, BEL, and Aduni
Our languages are confused. An important sign that we are in the extreme time of the end is described not only by Danial 12, but many other prophecies.

TsefanYahu (Zephaniah) 3:9 says a correction in our speech comes with a specific purpose:
"For by the fire of My jealousy all the arets shall be consumed. For then I shall turn to the peoples a clean lip, so that they all call on the Name of Yahuah, to serve Him with one shoulder." (BYNV eBook / Kindle)
Note the purpose: *"so that they all call on the Name of Yahuah, to serve Him with one shoulder."*
Because some meditate on His Name (Mal. 3), and they know His Name (Ps. 91), Yahuah will deliver them, and call them His treasured possession. Yahusha's bride knows her Husband's Name, she has stored the oil (a good Name) in her lamp. The unwise (without Torah) will be astonished that the door will not be opened to them at His sudden return.
"I am Yahuah your Alahim" is the 1st Commandment, but teachers fail to teach His Covenant, paving a broad road to destruction, but well-funded from fleecing and tickling the ears of their prey.

The Name Yahuah Is Like Perfume

The Song of Shalomoh 1:3 relates the scent of sweetness the bride senses when the Name of her Husband is spoken.

"Your Name is as oil (perfume) *poured out."*

Miriam poured a large amount of expensive perfume over Yahusha's feet, and wiped them with her hair six days before Pesak. (Yn. 12:3)

Another record of this event is found at Mt. 26:6-13.

At 2 Korinthians 2:15-16 Paul describes how Yahusha in us is a sweet fragrance to Yahuah, and to one another, but to those perishing we have the scent of death on us.

Forgive & Comfort One Another

2 Korinthians 2 guides us in how to be sensitive to others that will not turn from their error. We assure them of our love, and move on. We all see splinters jutting-out of each others' eyes, and often endure some very harsh attacks from individuals.

We have to press on toward the higher calling of being in the first resurrection as Yahusha's bride, and resist tromping all over each other when we feel offended or rejected. Just endure *silently.*

There's far too much grief caused by malicious attacks on the Internet. I feel grieved all the time as self-righteous people spread venomous gossip against one another with obvious malicious intent.

Only with Yahusha's help can we overcome the fleshly tendencies that trigger us. Stay courageous and revere no one but Yahusha; it's Him we serve, not men. Praise from men counts for nothing; we seek only the smile on Yahusha's face by doing what pleases Him. The Shepherd of Yisharal is watching you! (See Psalm 80)

The Afterlife

What happens to us after our body dies?

Most people choose to listen to a guru, rabbi, or respected spiritual leader they trust when seeking answers for fulfillment. These sources mainly want to control and **gaslight*** those who listen to them. Alternatively, we can believe the Word of Yahuah, and put all our trust in what He says. The term "gaslight" is a modern-day term describing psychological manipulation. It may or may not be intentional, but it causes someone to doubt their own perceptions of reality.

Yahusha made us in two main parts, the physical body, and the nefesh or living being dwelling in the body directing its behavior. This is His "breath of life," and it belongs to Him. At Mt. 10:28, Yahusha describes "both" of these components, and how only one is vulnerable to attack. One of these components can be easily destroyed, but the other can only be destroyed by the One that created it. No other created being can injure or kill the nefesh, so there is nothing further they can achieve than destroying the physical.

A suicide is a murderous act, however only Yahusha knows the inner torture a person is enduring to cause them to take such an extreme act against themselves. Only the One Who descended from Shamayim has ascended (Yahukanon 3:13, Acts 2:34), and His Name is Yahusha. We hear teachers saying the phrase, "go to heaven," but the Earth was created for our habitation, and will be inherited by those who receive their immortal bodies. He spoke to the beings whose bodies perished in the Flood while He was in sheol (1 Peter 3:18-20; the grave, abode of the dead). The nefesh of all people who are in sheol await their new incorruptible bodies, or await their final judgment, eternal death in yam aish. Where, why, how, when, and who are questions only Yahusha can answer because they are His to do with as He sees fit. All belong to Him, and we have to be careful how we make judgments about the dead, and the living as well. All things work together for good to those who love Yahuah, and are called according to His purpose (Romans 8:28).

Romans 8:39 explains that even death cannot separate us from the love of Alahim that is in Mashiak Yahusha, our Yahuah!

Just as the first man and woman were *gaslighted** by the dragon in Gan Eden, today's dimmed masses are being led into great darkness by *religious rituals* and *futile traditions* by those who teach them. The instructions of love are the Ten Commandments, and Yahusha referred to them when asked how one may gain eternal life (Mt. 19). The confusion is caused by teachers who misunderstand the old covenant involved animal blood, and the priesthood that offered it (Heb. 8:13, Dt. 31:26). Hebrews 8 explains that covenant is now obsolete, and was written on a SCROLL and placed beside the ark, **not inside** (Dt. 31:26). The Ten Words on the stone tablets are the ETERNAL Covenant, and these guide our hearts to do what is pleasing to Yahuah, and that begins by knowing and using His Name, which the first Commandment tells us: ANOKI YAHUAH ALAHIK . . . *"I am Yahuah your Alahim."* Read 1 Yahukanon / 1 John 2:4, and Yahusha's Spirit will pierce the heart of everyone who hears what He is saying, not what filters through the traditional teachings.
*What is *gaslighting*, and how do you know if it is happening to you?
Psychologists use the term gaslighting to refer to a specific type of manipulation where the manipulator is trying to get someone else (or a group of people) to question their own reality, memory or perceptions. Christian pastors use this technique to psycholocally manipulate their adherents.

The term gaslighting comes from a 1938 play, *Gaslight*. The play was turned into a more widely known movie in 1944, Gaslight, where a husband manipulates his wife to make her think she's losing her sense of reality so he can commit her to a mental institution and steal her inheritance.
This reminds us of what occurred in Gan Eden. The dragon tricked the woman into touching and eating the fruit of the forbidden tree. In modern terminology, this was an example of malicious gaslighting.

At Your Immersion, You Accept The Covenant
Obedience is not optional, it is essential to find the path to eternal life (Mt. 19:16-22).
Even demons believe Yahusha atoned for sin.
He did not come to destroy His Commandments, He came to destroy the works of the devil. His Commandments are not the works of the devil, but the Truth has been maligned and spoken of as evil (2 Peter 2:2). Those who teach "unconditional" love (that is, without repenting and turning back to obedience) have not yet read Hebrews 10 and 1 Yahukanon 2:4. The Name of Yahusha, and the walk He walked, are the mission He gave the first Natsarim - and now His last Natsarim are rising up all over the Earth.

FINDING TRUTH BEGINS BY SEEKING IT

Many people have been taught errors by teachers
using cartoons or something similar. All the Hindu
deities are cartoons, and Catholicism portrays what
they teach using stained glass and frescoes.
New thinking emerged from the period known as the
Renaissance. Newton, Copernicus and Galileo
paved the way for new branches of science.
Woodcuts and other illustrations from the period

show a disc shaped Earth with a domed half-sphere holding the Sun, Moon, and stars.

Copernicus theorized that the Earth circles the Sun, called *Heliocentricity*. Galileo proved this by observation, and published his findings, resulting in his arrest by cardinal Bellarmine, trial by the Inquisition, and excommunication from the Circus in 1633. His life was spared because he recanted what was considered heresy. All his research was banned, and he remained under house arrest until his death 8 years later. The irrational fear that almost resulted in Galileo being burned at the stake was finally acknowledged in 1979. Galileo was posthumously reinstated into the Circus.

If illustrations / cartoons are necessary to teach, it is because there is no real evidence. When we teach the Name of Yahuah, we show the physical evidence to validate it. Are cartoons going to validate the Truth? Not very likely. We have to accept one another as followers of Yahusha, but discussing our favorite understanding of the donut, cookie, meatball, or distances to Alpha Centauri are not the agenda of Yahusha. Way too much time is spent on how the physical universe is arranged, as if fixing the curtains on the Titanic might help people as they are wondering why the ship is lilting as it sinks. We're either on task and doing Yahusha's real work, or stopping to look at other people doing their work, and distracting them. It's very interesting to see the art from the past, and how it was used to deceive people for centuries.

Never Underestimate The Sneakiness Of The Dragon

Is Earth spherical, or flat with a half-sphere dome embedded with all the lights? What we believe about the geometry of Yahuah's Earth and Shamayim should never be the basis for divisions, yet many find it a basis for our deliverance. It's what we believe about the blood of Yahusha that matters most. Love is the goal, and *Yahuah's purpose for creating us is to select companions to live eternally with Him.* The whole world is deceived by the dragon, and they easily fall for cartoon deities as if they are real. Everything we see is passing away, and everything we cannot see is eternal (2 Korinthians 4:18).

WHAT IS SHEKINAH?

If you're looking for a great name for a book, movie, or a base in outer space, this might just be the one. The Shekinah is the dwelling place of the Name. (There can be only One: YAHUAH).
The root for the word MISHKAN (H4908) is SHAKAN (H7931) and means to abide or dwell. Adding the feminine suffix, we arrive at the unused word, SHEKINAH.

Why did Mushah's face glow? Why was light appearing above the heads of the first Natsarim on Shabuoth at Acts 2? Speaking to Mushah, what did Yahuah mean by "My Name is in him" when He referred to the pillar of cloud that glowed brightly from the tent of meeting? Danial 12 speaks of a glowing aspect on people who lead many to righteousness. The word SHEKINAH is not a word in the Writing of Truth. It's feminine form of the root of MISHKAN, a word often used. The temporary and movable *Dwelling Place* (MISHKAN) once was in the wilderness for the Presence of Yahuah to dwell among His people.

Mythical creatures named Shekinah aren't based in reality, although may have been used by storytellers in the past. Elon Musk may one day use the word SHEKINAH to name a Space-X station, a rocket, or a base on another planet.

https://youtu.be/PCslzi06FIQ (click for more)

The Call

Yahusha calls us to Himself, and He loved us first. He teaches us how to forgive because He forgave us first. He's first in all things, and He's awakening ambassadors all over the world to announce his coming. May His will be done on Earth, let's not pray to Him to do our will. All things work together for good to those who love Yahuah and are called according to His purpose.

Before you pray, make certain you obey Yahusha's Commandments. Calling on a false name and being disobedient to Yahusha's Commandments means your prayers are an abomination to Him. Proverbs 28:9 confirms this. Test everything with the Word. Look up this psychological-abuse term: *GASLIGHTING.* There are some people who do this to everyone around them, and often build-up a kind of gang-mentality against "others" they focus too much on. When you realize this kind of abuse has been used on you, the abuser's attempts to control, blame, or judge you becomes obvious. As Yahusha said, ***"If you abide in My Word, you are truly My disciples, and you will know the Truth, and the Truth will set you free."*** [Yahukanon 8:31-32] By their fruits you will know them. Do not be deceived by them.

The Jesuit Order is called **Societas IESV**.
Jesus is an altered term invented less than 500 years ago by Jesuits. The first edition of the KJV was based on the *Latin Vulgate*, and the term IESV was the device the Anglican Catholic Circus used to refer to Yahusha. This IESV was transferred directly from the Latin Vulgate. In place of Yahuah, the Latin Vulgate replaced the true Name with Dominus, which means LORD. Yahukanon (Yahuah is kindness) is what they now call the book of John. Thank you for replying, may you be restored to favor to Yahuah by your belief in the blood of Yahusha which redeems all those who repent and are immersed calling on His Name.

Yahuah is Yahusha, and He is coming to reign here on the Earth. The false teachings will all be wiped away. He said, "I am the Vine; you are the Natsarim (branches)." He also said, "You will not see Me again until you say, "BARUK HABA BASHEM YAHUAH!" (see Ps. 118:26).
The Lamb is coming in His real Name, not a fake one invented by Jesuits.
The crowd around us may put us in a narcotic state and cause us to believe we have found Truth, but when we take our first steps to walk in the way Yahusha walked, the foggy stupor disperses, and He lifts us out of it.
https://youtu.be/s4UN-tJleMl

TIRED OF LIES?

We should all grow tired of lies. If Yahusha never celebrated His birth, and was not born on December 25, why do we stand by and let the lie continue? Are sacraments real, or pretend? Is Constantine's edict to transfer the obligation to rest from the 7th day of each week to his Day of the Sun something we should accept, or reject as a lie? Yahusha refers to severe distress in the last days, and to pray we don't have to flee on the Sabbath at Mt. 24:20. Was He referring to the real Sabbath, or the newer one Constantine made up? There are dozens of other lies many have lived and died believing. I was taught to *talk to dead people* (necromancy) to make up for breaking the Commandments, but finally realized that was far worse than anything I ever sought forgiveness for. We are in a period of awakening, and it's because Danial 12 and Yual / Joel 2 are being fulfilled. Yahusha is pouring out His Spirit on all flesh, and many are being taught obedience, and this refining process is leading many to abandon all lies, and do what is pleasing to Yahusha, Who is Yahuah incarnate. He is at the door, and the trap is about to spring shut. Repent;

for the reign of Yahuah draws near. We will not see Him again, until we say,
"BARUK HABA BASHEM YAHUAH."
Challenge the pastors who teach tradition based on lies. Resist the father of lies, and his workers.

Eventually the Truth was overwhelmed by unconverted people who changed the Name of the One we serve, and all that He commanded us to obey. The whole world has gone mad on the wine of Babel.
We should use every opportunity to share our belief in Yahusha with those who will hear. However, to adopt a framework of witchcraft to illustrate His teachings would be unlikely to get His approval (such as trees, wreaths, Santa, eggs, bunnies, and other fertility symbols used by pagans).

CONSTANTINE'S CREED
"I renounce all customs, rites, legalisms, unleavened breads and sacrifices of lambs of the Hebrews, and all the other festivals of the Hebrews, sacrifices, prayers, aspirations, purifications, sanctifications, and propitiations, fasts and new moons, Sabbaths, superstitions, hymns and chants, observances. and assemblies. Absolutely everything Yahudi, every law, rite, and custom, and if afterwards I shall wish to deny and return to Yahudim superstition, or shall be found eating with Yahudim, or feasting with them, or secretly conversing and condemning the Christian religion instead of openly confuting them and condemning their vain faith, then let the trembling of Cain and the leprosy of Gehazi cleave to me, as well as the legal punishments to which I acknowledge myself

liable. And may I be an anathema in the world to come, and may my soul be set down with satan and the devils."

Natsarim wishing to join this "holy community" were compelled to adopt a different set of rules and customs. All new members were to take this oath:

"I accept all customs, rites, legalism, and feasts of the Romans' sacrifices. Prayers, purifications with water, sanctifications by Pontificus Maxmus (high priests of Rome), propitiations, and feasts, and the New Sabbath "Dies Solis" (Day of the Sun, all new chants and observances, and all the foods and drinks of the Romans. I absolutely accept everything Roman, every new law, rite and custom, of Rome, and the New Roman Religion."

In approximately 365 AD, the Council of Laodicea made all Natsarim anathema:

"Christians must not Judaize by resting on the Sabbath, but must work on that day. Rather, honoring the Lord's Day. But if any shall be found to be Judaizers, let them be anathema (separated) from Christ."

Note: Protestants are included as they still observe the holidays and Sabbath of Rome. Would this make Yahusha separated from Himself? He referred to the day at Mt. 24:20, telling us to pray we not be forced to flee on that day.

"To the Torah and to the Witness; If they do not speak according to this Word, it is because they have no daybreak." (YashaYahu 8:20)

WORMWOOD -How To Recognize False Teachings

A truths initial commotion is directly proportional to how deeply the lie was believed... When a well-packaged web of lies has been sold gradually to the masses over generations, the truth will seem utterly preposterous and its speaker, a raving lunatic. -Dresden James
"If you abide in My Word, you are truly my disciples, and you will know the Truth, and the Truth will set you free." Yn. 8:31-32
https://www.amazon.com/gp/product/154862857 3/ref=dbs_a_def_rwt_bibl_vppi_i34
Look-Inside-the-book at Amazon

Yahusha in us makes it possible to recognize good or bad Torah (instruction). The only Deliverer and Judge is Yahusha. Individuals who determine the outcome of others make themselves above Torah (the eternal Covenant). By the measure they use to judge, they will be judged. If we have properly understood YashaYahu (Isaiah) 8:20 & 51:7, we must first know what is upright (Yahuah's instructions) and that we do not fear the revilings of men. We can determine "good Torah" and "bad Torah" (instructions, teaching). Behavior is the good or bad fruit from what instructions a person accept as Truth. If anyone knows Yahusha, they guard His Commandments. If they claim to know Him, but do not guard them, they are liars. (1 Yn. 2:4). Most people are following the dragon into oblivion, and that's why Natsarim teachings sound ridiculous to them. The Natsarim have always been accused of being heretics by the circus fathers, yet are the original followers of Yahusha. Remember, Yahusha said, *"I am the Vine, you are the Natsarim."*

The Magisterim's traditions are adapted pagan customs, re-invented to mask their original origins. The late 4th century Latin Vulgate was exclusively used by the Universal Circus (Catholic Church) for 1200 years (a period aligned with the Dark Ages). The Latin word **Dominus** replaced the Name of Yahuah in the Latin Vulgate. Today, the primary transliteration for the Tetragrammaton we find in dictionaries and encyclopedias is the spelling **Yahweh**. Closer research reveals the error of the letter "**double-U**," a letter invented by a typesetter after 1450 CE. Gutenburg's largest print job required the Latin Vulgate to be printed one page at a time, and the letter **V** in Latin operated as our modern letter **U**, so a typesetter invented a double letter which combined two into one, producing the **VV**. More is explained here:
http://www.fossilizedcustoms.com/transliteration.html

What Is The Tree Of Life?
It's mentioned at the beginning, in the middle, and at the end of the Scriptures. It is the life-giving Word of Yahuah men seek, but those who teach them have kept them from finding it. The *Way of Truth* is maligned and spoken of as *evil* (2Peter 2:2). ***"Your Word is a lamp to my feet, and a Light to my path."*** - Psalm 119:105

Who Is Restraining Who?
The restrainer is the evil one, not the Ruach ha Qodesh (Spirit of Yahusha). The restrainer will be taken out of the way when Yahusha returns. The false teachings of Christianity have everyone disobeying the everlasting Covenant.

Yahusha is activating His ENDTIME WATCHMEN
Run to Yahusha, the Fountain of Living Waters!
Everyone in agreement with each video is
responsible for sharing them because people are
perishing and drowning in lies. Notice all the videos
that teach nothing of vital importance, but are
window dressing on a sinking ship. "To the Torah
and to the Witness! If they do not speak according
to this Word, it is because they have no daybreak!"
[YashaYahu 8:20]
https://youtu.be/DL_84PSdUsE

Copy & Paste above text and share with all your
contacts and other media.

Catholic Bishops giving the Nazi salute in honor of Hitler, future Pope
Benedict in the Center brown suit Nazi

Why Everyone Is Freaking-Out

The whole world is being controlled by the media, and the media is controlled by the Jesuit-Illuminati, and the Jesuit-Illuminati is controlled by the controller, the dragon.

We are controlled by Yahusha.

There is a pressure to stifle information by "BIG TECH" (all the big ones that come to mind, especially the four horsemen, Amazon, Apple, Google, Facebook), or Tech Giants.

"Let not your heart be troubled. Believe in Alahim, believe also in Me. In My Father's house there are many rooms. And if not, I would have told you. I go to prepare a place for you.
And if I go and prepare a place for you, I shall come again and receive you to Myself, that where I am, you might be too." Yahukanon 14:1-3

We bear the seal of Yahusha, and are armored. Our only offensive weapon is His Name, the Word that He will bring about the fall of Babel.
We will prevail while others will cower in fear, because we know His Name.
He often encouraged His chosen ones who wondered how they could possibly endure what they were told to do with these words:
"Because I am with you."

I Still Remember What Startled Me Awake
The Jesuit-Illuminati teaches *"the end justifies the means."* I was educated by them, but I did not trust them. They explained the World Order as a means of control, but this phase, *"the end justifies the means,"* was the moment I realized the evil behind those who taught me. Everything they taught was programming to steer a young child's thinking processes to become a mindless drone. Only Yahusha can awaken a mind to perceive the Truth, and He does this by instilling a love for His Word in us.
https://www.youtube.com/user/LewWhite10/videos

THE BEAST
The *world order* was explained to me by the beast itself, and for the first 18 years of my life I was a part of it. The Jesuits explained how this beast controls the world. The 3 estates (eschelons, levels, principalities) in which all the beast's authority is arranged are:
CLERGY
NOBILITY
LAITY

The Societas IESV (Jesuit order) focuses on programming their drones at the earliest possible age, so they can imprint the child's thinking processes to conform to their control.
Ignatius Loyola (founder of the Societas IESV) said, ***"Give us a child till he's seven and we'll have him for life."***

Catholic altar boys are in all sorts of danger. In my years as an altar boy, they made me serve in a black cassock like Rasputin (or a Buddhist monk). They taught me Latin, and conformity to processes which took many years to purge from my mind. The circus show is really a staged play, with rituals performed to mesmerize the audience. The incense is surely enhanced with psycho-active ingredients. The things they do are adopted from Hinduism (like halos, steeples, bells, candle trays, statues, bowing, and water splashing). Even the prayer beads are a form of divination and necromancy (prayers to the dead), which also came from the Hindu trinity (Brahma-Uishnu-Shiba), and are seen on Shiba statues. It all reached the Middle East around 200 BCE, from the Silk Road trade route out of India.

The reign of Babel is the World Order at present, but its end is near.

Why do Judges wear black robes?

The primary reason for their costumes is tradition, but few realize the origins of what they do.
The black robes are very ancient garments worn by the dark robed priests (KOMARIM) engaged in Sun worship.
These robes are also called cassocks, and are also worn by sophists. Rasputin is pictured wearing the same dark robe shared by Jesuits and Catholic altar boys.
Most Mystagogues controlling teachings (aka, Nikolaitanes) wear sophistry costumes like cassocks, and may be various colors.
The Dalai Lama is one example of this.

Got Crescent Yoga Stance?

Yoga / yoking is not widely recognized for what it is, but it is a component, or practice, originating in training exercises from Hinduism. Eastern mysticism uses many avenues to make darkness appear as light. It may be alright with the LORD our GOD, but Yahuah our Alahim instructs us not the learn the ways of the heathen. If we draw closer to Yahusha, He will draw closer to us. If we love Him, we will guard His Commandments; but performing yoga postures on a magic carpet was never mentioned to show our love for Him.

Silk Road Stuff

The sitting position (asana) is recognized around the world as a meditation technique called yoga (yoking). The Hindu culture promotes an assortment of teachings that spread along the Silk Road as India swelled to reach the Middle East around 200 BCE. Consulting guides for training in how to align one's shakras, the use of mudras, mats, domes, circumambulating, yoking / yoga, and many other features of Gnosticism have used modern technologies to engage the human imagination.

Kirlian photography and mood rings have been lures for the simple who are told their aura is an indicator they need to pay attention to. The folded legs when sitting (asana) is not comfortable, but is a serpentine form, as if one is sitting on a large coil of serpents. Serpent wisdom, the mudras (hand gestures), and chants are ancient methods used to invite demonic possession to the unwary. Manipulation of forces is witchcraft. Gurus train their followers to perform *namaste* (folded hands), a way of expressing the following message: *"my spirit bows to the spirit in you."*

Any one of these things is in direct violation of the 1st, 2nd, and 3rd Commandments of lovingkindness, and makes one guilty of idolatry. Promising *fulfillment* through false wisdom, their goal is to reach nirvana (oblivion), and forsake the purpose of their Creator, eternal life with Him as His companion. Ephesians 5:11 says, "Have no fellowship with the fruitless deeds of darkness, but rather expose them."

"To the Torah and to the Witness; if they do not speak according to this Word, it is because they have no daybreak." - YashaYahu / Isaiah 8:20

For more:

http://www.fossilizedcustoms.com/yoke.html

ESOTERIC FORCES

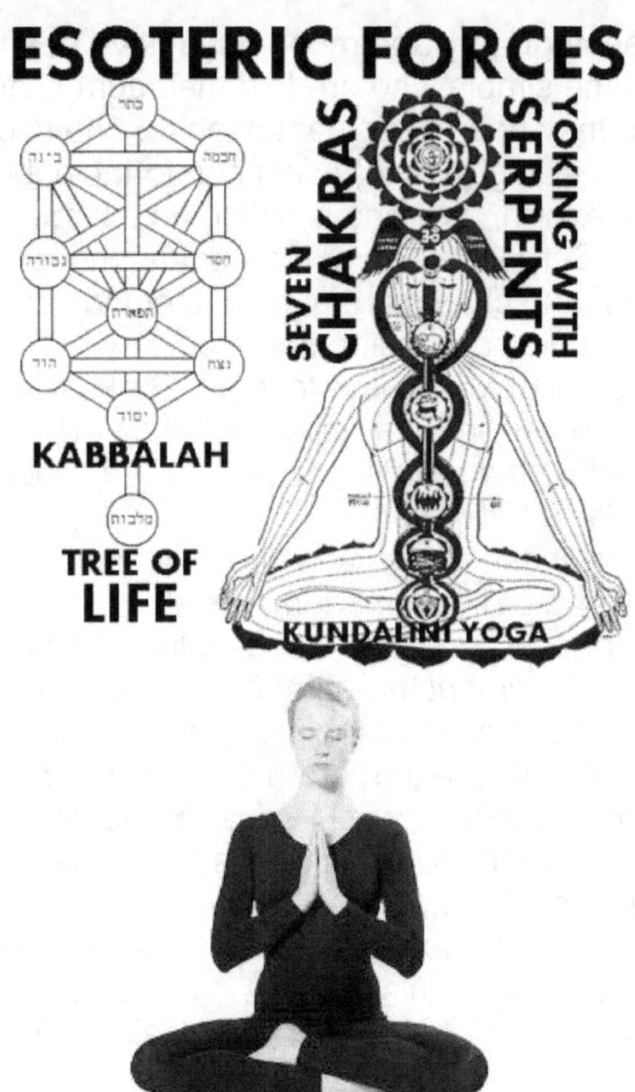

Bowing Down To The Host Of Heaven?

They need to hear the Truth. Passover is once a year, at its proper time in the first month of the year (Shemoth / Exodus 12:2). They are persuaded by men's traditions to meet on each first day of the week in the morning, calling it a supper. The rituals of men alter the Word of Yahuah, and their behavior is the reason Yahuah is about to unleash His fiery wrath on the inhabitants of the Earth (YashaYahu / Is. 24). HOC EST CORPUS MEUM (this is my body in Latin) cannot alter any substance, but the Word of Yahuah teaches the way to become His body, so walk in it.

GEORGIA GUIDESTONES

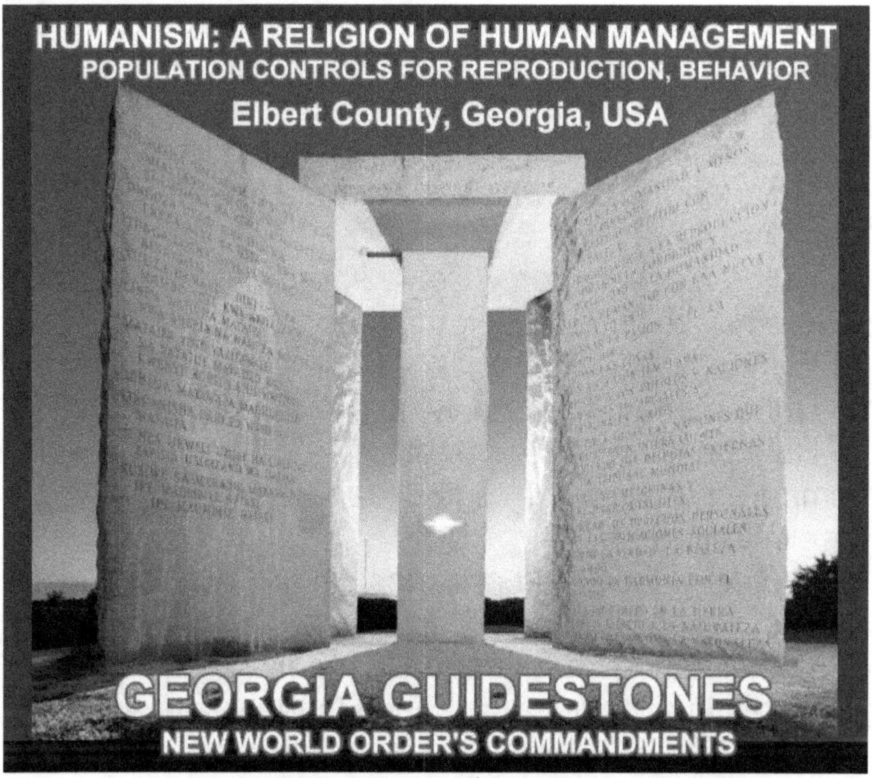

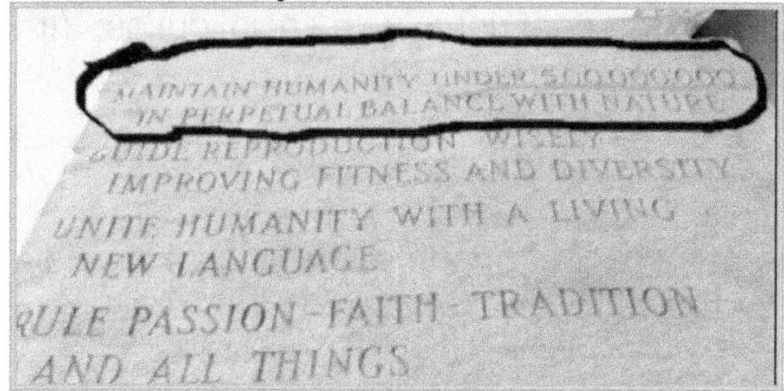

Look carefully at the 1st commandment:

Humanists' Ten Commandments
(Georgia Guidestones):
1. Maintain humanity under 500,000,000 in perpetual balance with nature. (Note that item #1 is about population control - for a sustainable, equitable, manageable society. This is why ABORTION is such a huge issue for them to keep legal. They will have to murder much more than the unborn to achieve their goals. They are concerned about the limited natural resources and current rates of consumption, so they are going to foment viral pandemics, to which a selected few will be immune).
2. Guide reproduction wisely - improving fitness and diversity.   (Notice this wording softens the idea of EUGENICS).
3. Unite humanity with a living new language.
4. Rule passion - faith - tradition - and all things with tempered reason.   (religious fanatics will be cured or eliminated).
5. Protect people and nations with fair laws and just courts.
6. Let all nations rule internally resolving external disputes in a world court. The Hague is already the NWO court.
7. Avoid petty laws and useless officials.
8. Balance personal rights with social duties. (If you don't produce, you're a burden, and must be eliminated - cleansed).
9. Prize truth - beauty - love - seeking harmony with the infinite.
10. Be not a cancer on the earth - Leave room for nature - Leave room for nature.

The Reign Of Yahusha Is Coming

The burning wrath on the Day of Yahuah will punish the inhabitants of the Earth. Those who **repent** and are **immersed** calling on the Name of **Yahusha** are sealed for the day of our redemption. Christians are taught to disobey, not live (abide) in the Word. Natsarim were instructed to teach the nations the Name, and teach them to guard all the Commandments we were to guard.

What was the Old Covenant? What is the Renewed Covenant?

One was animal blood, the second was the blood of Yahusha.

Here's the Besorah (message):

Repent - turn from men's teachings and traditions. Turn back to the eternal Covenant.

The reign of Yahusha draws near. Teach the Name of Yahuah, and instruct everyone to obey all things we were instructed to obey (Commandments and appointed times given at Ex. 20 / Dt. 5, and Dt. 16). The change in the priesthood (offering animal blood) is all that's been done away with, so don't rebuild a place to do those things. Yahusha did not come to destroy His Torah; He came to destroy the works of the devil.

One cannot repent and simultaneously think they can live as if the Ten Commandments no longer matter.

REDEMPTION

We are transformed by trusting only in the blood of Yahusha. The renewed Covenant in His blood cancels the penalty of death for our sins. It makes the old covenant obsolete. The old covenant was the animal blood offered by the former priests, and the instructions were hand-written on a scroll and placed beside the ark – see Dt. 31:26. The old covenant is not the Ten Commandments, nor the Scriptures (Genesis to Malaki), although this is what the world has been programmed to believe. Even demons believe. We should not listen to men's interpretations, but read the Word for ourselves. The Truth will set us free from men's puffed-up ideas (leaven).

Can we know what a book is about without reading it? People have told me how they know all about the Scriptures of Truth because someone told them all about it. They had never read it for themselves.

A Tenth Of Your Increase

The tithe (a tenth of our increase) is food and given to the old covenant priesthood to be used to support the widow, fatherless, disabled and poor, and foreigners fleeing or passing through. Most of the burden for caring for the poor and aged folks fell on their relatives (Yaqub 2:15).

At Barashith 14:18-20, we see the first occurrence of "a tenth" being given to Melkizedeq. The phrase we read literally says, ***"Then Abram gave him a tenth of everything."***

Malaki 3:10 mentions gathering food for the storehouse. Yahuah said to withhold the tithe was robbing Him.

Other than the tithe of food collected by the former priesthood, alms were collected by the poor directly. Cornelius, a gentile centurion described at Acts 10, gave alms to the poor. At Acts 3, a man born lame was doing this at the Beautiful Gate. Occasionally land or houses were sold, and the proceeds given to the emissaries for supporting those in need (Acts

4).
The Natsarim served food for the needy at tables (Acts 6), and elders who worked well at teaching the Word were worthy of a double portion (of food).
Our close relatives and brothers and sisters in dire need of essentials for living are the recipients of all giving, but too often the support is mostly used for buildings set up to teach the traditions of men.
Yahusha said "feed My sheep" at Yn. 21, and by this He meant to teach them to obey, not steal their food.

Be Careful How You Listen
We are instructed to guard the Commandments, and by doing this we will be blessed, but our obedience doesn't earn eternal life - we were purchased with the precious blood of Yahusha our Redeemer.
The severing of the Scriptures into two parts was done by Marcion of Sinope (85-160 CE). The tenth part (tithe) is very dear to lawless teachers who do not teach the Commandments, yet they expect to receive the whole tithe in the form of money from those whose itching ears are being scratched. We should support the needy in our family, the poor nearby, and give to support teachers who serve the body of Yahusha well. Those who do not teach the Commandments do not know Yahusha. 1 Yn. 2:3-4

How Friday the 13th Became A THING
An Excerpt from the book Fossilized Customs 12th Edition:
FRI-DAY THE THIRTEENTH
"Preparation Day" is a term for every sixth day of the week. It is also used to refer to any day prior to

an annual appointed time. Six of the seven annual appointments are movable, one of which is the **1st Day of Matsah**, or Unleavened Bread. Obviously, there are not **3 DAYS AND 3 NIGHTS** between "Fri-Day" night at sunset and "Sun-Day" morning. Shatan's spin-doctors twisted it for us so that a Sunday morning "supper" they instituted would justify the old pagan **day of the Sun**.

Pagans assembled to worship the Sun in the morning on the first day of the week. Because the entire Christian world has been programmed to believe the day of Yahusha's **resurrection** is permanently affiliated with the first day of the week, they do not observe Passover. Shatan bruised the heel of Yahusha. The myth that Yahusha died on a "Fri-Day," and not the preparation day for the High Shabath of Matsah (Yn. 19:31) is part of the superstition of <u>Fri-Day the 13th</u>. The "13" represents the fact that there were **13 MEN** present at the meal the previous evening. The 13th day of each Roman month has no connection with the real moon, nor the number of men present at the meal. Not only that, but what day the resurrection occurred has nothing to do with what DAY is the Shabath, our day of rest. It's hard to understand how the smoke-and-mirrors masked so much of the truth, and could be propagated by so many scholars over so many centuries. Shatan successfully blinded the eyes of populations with his teachers, and desolated the correct pattern of observances.

When Was Yahusha Born?
Passover is a shadow of Yahusha's *death*, not His *birth*. The idea that Yahusha was born in the early Spring when lambs' birth rates peak sounds

plausible, but Yahusha's birth is more associated with Sukkoth, and His circumcision on the 8th day. Shepherds watch over their flocks day and night, but especially to protect them from night-stalking predators, not primarily to watch for lambing. Equivocating can be unintentionally associating dissimilar but coincidental occurrences, very much like Christianity has adopted the rebirth of the Sun as the birthday of Yahusha. See more details online at this link:
http://www.fossilizedcustoms.com/birth.html

Yahusha And The Commandments vs. The Dragon
The mission He ordered to be done by His Natsarim has been resisted by the dragon. Our mission is to hunt and fish for the lost, and feed them the message of Truth; that is, to guard the Name and Commandments we were given to guard and obey. The dragon is not happy about this (Rev. 12:17). For those who are called, the differences in the words we use will be overcome by Yahusha's purification process over time. The overcoming of the world is found in our belief, following no one else but the Word of Yahuah, Yahusha Himself. Our love for one another is how the world will identify us. Yahusha identifies us in this way: "ANI HA GAFEN; ATAH HA NATSARIM." (I am the Vine; you are the Natsarim).
To determine if you are on the right path to eternal life, read 1 Yn. 2:4 to test whether or not you know Yahusha. If you don't, you may be under the control of the dragon, and not know it yet. This is your chance to take the red pill.

What Is Torah?

Torah is a mirror that reflects how we appear to its standard of perfection (See Yaqub 1:24).
It teaches us how to walk before Yahuah, and do the things that please Him.
This is what Hillel said to the guy (gentile) who wanted to be taught the whole Torah while standing on one foot:
"What is hateful to you, do not do to your neighbor. The rest is commentary, go and learn."

The Riddle Concerning Buying & Selling

Wisdom is Torah. Wisdom enables a person to discern when not to buy and sell. The ones not having wisdom have been taught Torah does not control their behavior, so they buy and sell everyday. They are told "everyday is Sabbath." Torah keeps us from violating the day Yahuah has set-apart, and it is the mark of the eternal Covenant (Ex. 31:13, Ez. 20:12). Revelation 13 is related as a riddle, but the ones without wisdom cannot discern the solution to the riddle.
http://www.fossilizedcustoms.com/mark.html

How To Detect The Beast

The reign of Babel is an organized power structure made up of 3 estates, or principalities:
1. Clergy (head, controller); 2. Nobility (world governments): 3. Laity (common people, think and do what they are told). Gabriel explained it to Danial as 4 beasts. The riddle of the mark at Revelation 13 cannot be solved (calculated) concerning buying and selling without wisdom. Wisdom is Torah (instructions). The reign of Babel is controlled by the dragon, and goes against Torah at every turn, and

wages war against those who obey the Commandments of Yahuah, and testify that Yahuah is Yahusha our Deliverer.

The sign of the eternal Covenant is the 4th of the Ten Commandments (Ez. 20:1-49). The reign of Yahusha comes as the 7th messenger announces Him (Rev. 11). The Torah keeps us from buying and selling, one day each week; not the beast. The Clergy announced the sign of their authority is the change of the 4th Commandment, fulfilling Danial 7:25. When a little wisdom goes around the authoritarian controller and the common people detect they have been deceived, we see the dragon become enraged. This prompts the Jesuit-Illuminati to action, resulting in arrests, book burnings, inquisitions, ethnic cleansing, secret political meetings with the pope, all focusing on restoring power to the wounded head of the 4th beast. Guard the 4th Commandment, and solve the riddle.

The Eternal Covenant of Love is unchanged because Yahuah is trustworthy, and mankind is not. When Yahusha told us to pray that our flight not be in winter of on a Shabath day, He was describing the extreme last days of the reign of Babel (see Mt. 24:20). Many are taught to ignore the first 4 Commandments, and the last 6 still define sin, but they are being misled. They will buy and sell on the Shabath day, believing it moved to the first day. We understand the riddle at Rev. 13, having wisdom from the Torah to know when we are not to buy and sell. Christianity outlawed resting on Shabath at their Council of Laodicea, resting on the first day as *Christians*.

Christianos is a Greek word from that time, meaning a retarded person (more about this word below).

We are *Natsarim* (Acts 24:5), as Yahusha said at Yn. 15:5, "I am the Vine, you are the Natsarim." Because I've brought up inquisitions, it may interest some to know the RCC killed and tortured millions of people over a period of 600 years. One of my favorite people in the study of the kosmos is Galileo Galilei. His research produced telescopes, thermometers, and an accurate understanding of things that disturbed the authoritarian controllers of information in his time.

Christian: What It Originally Meant

The original meaning and use of the Greek words Χριστιανός (Christianos, idiot) and Χριστός (Christos, meaning anointed) have been re-invented over a span of almost two millennia. Acts 24:4 identifies Yahusha's follower Paul as a "ringleader of the sect of the Natsarim," which Yahusha also called his followers at Yahukanon (John) 15:5. The modern word CRETIN traces back to the scornful Greek word, Χριστιανός. 1 Peter 4:15 lists terms we should not be known as (murderer, thief, evildoer, busybody, and Χριστιανός) but if we suffer by being labeled Χριστιανός (idiot), we should esteem Yahuah and not be ashamed. Originally, Χριστιανός did not mean "follower of Χριστός."

Christianos: The Real Meaning Of The Word

Outsiders (not Natsarim) called us christianos at first at Antioch (Acts 11:26). This was a term of scorn in that time, and has adopted a new meaning over time by revisionist teachings. The term christianos became the Latin form christianus. Look up the etymology of the word CRETIN. The original word it derives from is the word christianos. The

same word (christianos) is found at 1 Peter 4:15-16 among other terms one might be called by outsiders, and they are all shameful. Peter told Natsarim not to suffer as a murderer, thief, meddler in other's affairs, or any other sort of criminal. Peter knew the upright conduct of the Natsarim would bring insults, so he included the term christianos (simpleton, idiot, cretin). If they call us a christianos (cretin), we take it in stride, and praise Alahim for the persecution. Peter did not imply at any time that we called ourselves by this term; he included it in a list of other scornful labels. We know we are not christianos; Yahusha named us at Yahukanon 15:5: ***"I am the Vine; you are the Natsarim."***
ANI HA GAFEN; ATAH HA NATSARIM

The term CHRISTIANOS meant "idiot" in the mind of those Greeks that encountered the followers of Yahusha at Antioch. The term NATSARIM is prophetic (YirmeYahu / Jeremiah 31:6). The word ***Natsarim*** was used by an accuser who knew what we were really called (Acts 24:5). Revisionism caused the label "Christian" to become adopted, but they call themselves this now, not those of us trying to tell them the Truth. The Yahudim in the land of Israel call Christians "NOTSRIM," and the Arabs call Christians "NAZRANI," and we call ourselves "NATSARIM." The enemy knows what we are called, and we obey the Commandments of Alahim and hold to the testimony of Yahusha. Ask Yahusha if you should continue referring to His followers as Christianos, or Natsarim. Here is one of many etymological sources for the word CRETIN:
From French crétin ("cretin, idiot"), from crestin, an Alpine dialectal form of chrétien, from Vulgar Latin

__christiānus__ in the lost sense of "anyone in Christendom", often with a sense of "poor fellow".
The Latin source word is from Greek, CHRISTIANOS.
It is one of the terms in a list of other scornful labels at 1 Peter 4:15.

"I am the Vine; you are the Natsarim." - Yahukanon / John 15:5).
Knowledge of the Truth is increasing around the world as Danial 12 predicted.
Our teachers have led us into confusion - YashaYahu / Is. 9:16).
The guyim will come from the ends of the Earth and say, "Our fathers have inherited nothing but lies and futility" - YirmeYahu 16:19. We've heard many lies.

Who Is The Liar?
Yahusha said, "I am the Vine" (ANI HA GAFEN), "you are the Natsarim" (ATAH HA NATSARIM).
He called us Natsarim, the branches of His teachings. He told us to teach the guyim (nations) His Name, calling on it in their immersion for the forgiveness of their sins, and to teach those guyim to obey everything we were commanded to obey. Those doing this today are the Natsarim. We are not Christians. The dragon is enraged at those obeying the Commandments of Alahim, and testifying of Yahusha (Rev. 12:17). The one we obey is the one we are the servants of (Romans 6:16). The one who obeys the Commandments knows Yahusha (1 Yn. 2:4).
The one not guarding the Commandments, but claiming to know Yahusha, is a liar.

A Mark Of Confusion

The conflicted teachings we hear drive us to solve for clear answers. We were once deceived, so we understand how they were deceived. With Yahusha's guidance, we can patiently help them see the Truth. Hearing the Truth demands a response from each heart that hears it.

Do you agree there is confusion over what the mark of the beast is at Revelation 13? Can you offer any solution to the riddle that concerns wisdom, and how it relates to buying and selling? The Torah is wisdom, but without it the world will never figure out (interpret, calculate) the riddle correctly.

Wisdom tells us very clearly:

We are not to buy and sell on Shabath.

We also do not work, or make others work. Yahusha told His Natsarim, "And pray that your flight does not take place in winter, or on a Shabath." (see Mt. 24:20). There can be only one conclusion. It's Torah that prevents us from buying and selling, not the beast. When we meditate on Yahuah's Word, our minds find peace, and things work together for our good.

And Yet It Moves

The Sun we receive light and warmth from is an average-sized star. The Moon reflects the light from the Sun, causing the phases we see from our perspective on Earth. Sometimes the Moon passes between the Earth and Sun, eclipsing all or part of the Sun's photosphere. There are solar observatories both on Earth and in orbit that study the Sun constantly. The geometry of the objects, and their distance from Earth, has been known for thousands of years. Archimedes of Syracuse (3rd century BCE) was a student of physics, and worked out the sizes, shapes, and distances between the Earth, Sun, and Moon. Roman Catholicism's cardinal Bellarmine arrested Galileo and put him on trial before the Inquisition in 1633 for teaching his discoveries against Geocentrism. *Heliocentrism* was proclaimed to be heretical by the Inquisition.

To avoid torture and death, Galileo recanted his ideas that the Earth moves around the Sun (Copernican Theory of Heliocentricity). Legend says that after he stated the Earth does not move around the Sun, he whispered under his breath, *"And yet it moves."* His books and writings were banned, and was held under house arrest until his death eight years later.

Zetetic Kosmology (Greek, *zetetikos;* inquiring, questioning)

Our adversary is not flesh and blood, but works in the unseen realm to beguile and create divisions. Proponents of a flat Earth make it seem there is a conspiracy they need to expose, but these issues have no bearing on the mission given to Yahusha's Natsarim. Keep seeking Yahusha every day.

Geometry cannot deliver us, so I tend to leave it out of most discussions. I enjoy the imaginative designs of *zetetic kosmology*, but *real photographs* and video recordings of Yahuah's creation are so much better than cartoon drawings. Seducing spirits would like to waste our time with all kinds of arrogant nonsense. The geometric shape of the objects Yahuah has created should not be used as a stumbling block of any kind.

1 Korinthians 4:18: "So we fix our eyes not on what is seen, but on what is unseen. For what is seen is temporary, but what is unseen is eternal."

Stranger Shapes

Pizza and Donut cartoons showing odd shapes of the Earth are showing up all over the Internet. Voyager was launched In 1977 to send back all sorts of data, and dozens of other missions have increased knowledge since then. Gravitational lensing of dark matter have proven the existence of black holes in deep space within our galaxy. The center of the universe is fun to imagine, and fictional books represent almost 40% of all books sold in the world. Children's books represent 46%, religious books are 8%. Non-fiction books are only 7% of all books sold. These percentages may explain what the world is really infatuated with, and why people are so easily deceived.

https://www.torahzone.net/Flat-Earth-Hoax-pdf-download.html

What Is The Firmament?

The old English word firmament is rarely used or understood today. There are many new teachers of the "flat Earth" theory who have a Medieval concept of the skies (heavens, space, firmament), and in their mindset believe the word refers to a solid hemispherical dome that surrounds the flat Earth, and this dome has the stars, Sun, and Moon embedded in it somehow. The Eberith / Hebrew word, and it's context in the sentence, describes an expanse, or what we understand most simply as "space."

The word is RAQIA (**#7549**), and refers to a spatial expanse between the MAYIM, or waters (**#4325**). This word for waters is part of another word for skies: SHAMAYIM (**#8064**). For an historical perspective of how distortions of words caused misunderstandings about the Kosmos:

http://www.fossilizedcustoms.com/flatearth.html

"What is highly thought of among men is an abomination in the sight of Alahim." Luke 16:14-15

WILL CHRISTMAS SURVIVE?

This explosive revelation will not be accepted by many. People aren't hearing this, but pastors know it: Christmas was adopted from pagans, and Yahusha was not born on December 25th. Yahuah is our Alahim, and He became flesh to reconcile us to Himself, shedding His own precious blood to redeem us completely (Acts 20:28). Those who have pledged themselves to Him in immersion do not continue to sin against Him, otherwise they will will receive the judgment we read about at Hebrews 10. The Galatians were turning back to their former patterns, living as pagans (birthday cakes & wishes to the queen of heaven, special days, and all their highly esteemed holidays). They were turning away from the Truth, and were backsliding into the weak and miserable principles their parents had taught them. Today's pastors, teachers, and parents have all embraced these things, and train children to do the same. Who can stand before Yahusha when He comes to end all the idolatry we inherited from our fathers? Only His pure bride will be safely protected from the reapers as they burn the weeds first, then gather the wheat. Psalm 91 tells us we will see fiery wrath poured out on 10,000 at our right hand, but it will not come near our tent. The plagues are here, and the fire comes next. We're not getting this warning by listening to the majority of teachers. *They just put up more egg trees.*

People have no idea what "ornaments" really are. There's no room for Truth in today's dens of iniquity. Pastors know Yahusha was not born on December 25th or anytime near the solstice, but they remain silent about this error. They allow children to participate in stage plays that teach many inaccuracies (lies). The magi came two years after His birth, yet plays often depict them with the shepherds on the same night He was born. In their plays, the messenger telling Yusef to flee to Egypt pops up just after the Magi impart valuable gifts to sustain them while in Egypt. In reality, the magi visit was two years later. If Yusef took Yahusha to Egypt as quickly as the children's books tell the story, Yahusha would have missed His circumcision 8 days after He was born, and Yusef would have had plenty of gold to offer much more than two doves for the purification offering (Luke 2:28). If pastors taught the Truth, they would be unable to scratch the itching ears, so they keep the dream alive.

Halloween - After Yahusha Returns
While thinking with our old fleshly perspective, we can perceive what we're doing because we a spiritually dead (or drunk). The old wine gets emptied from us through a process performed by the indwelling Spirit of Yahusha, refining us to become like Him. It is no longer we who live, but Yahusha lives in us. Trick-or-treating, trunk-or-treating, birthday cakes, Sun-day morning steeple services, and literally everything cherished dearly by everyone will vanish, and never be remembered, when the reign of Yahusha comes to this Earth. The beginning is near, the branches (Natsarim) are beginning to blossom across the entire world.
https://youtu.be/G2ABkespQ7Y
The dragon is enraged at the woman, and is making war with her offspring who guard the Commandments of Alahim and testify of Yahusha.

How To Begin Following Yahusha

Our pledge (immersing in water) to obedience comes from inside us by the moving of our hearts by the Spirit of Yahusha. It comes from our own mouth, not an elder or anyone standing nearby. They cannot speak for us, nor can we speak to Yahusha through them.

Our repentance (turning back) from sin and obeying comes by hearing, then believing. We are called / chosen by Yahusha, not men and their traditions. Our response to His call is to go to the water, beg His forgiveness for our sins, and proclaim our belief in His blood given to purchase us. This is the moment of our circumcision, the outward pledge of a good conscience toward Alahim (that is, Yahusha).

"YAHUSHA, DELIVER ME!" – words our heart and mind scream out when we realize how much He loves us.

Yahusha is Hebrew, and means "I am your Deliverer."

Watch a short video:
https://www.youtube.com/watch?v=lr7eh_Yh4wo

I hope you run to Yahusha, and not a Nikolaitan.

Where Are The Lawless Teachers Paul Spoke Of?

2 Timothy chapters 2 through 4 speak of hard times in the last days. Teachers of lawlessness will multiply because people will not listen to sound doctrine, and they heap up for themselves teachers saying what they want them to say. Their "itching ears" are their spiritual ears, and only lawless teachers can scratch that itch.

Read 2 Timothy 4:1-4:

In the sight of Yahuah and Aduni Yahusha Mashiak, who shall judge the living and the dead at His appearing and His reign, I earnestly charge you: Proclaim the Word! Be urgent in season, out of season. Correct, warn, appeal, with all patience and teaching. For there shall be a time when they shall not bear sound teaching, but according to their own desires, they shall heap up for themselves teachers tickling the ear, and they shall indeed turn their ears away from the Truth, and be turned aside to myths." [sacraments, holy water, transubstantiation, Sunday, Trinities, celibacy, image worship, popes, nuns, monks, steeples, monstrances, chants, special days, lent, prayers to the dead, indulgences, pilgrimages, stigmatas, Easter eggs, December 25th Solstice birth, etc].

Acts 20:28-30:

"Keep watch over yourselves and the entire flock of which the Ruach haQodesh has made you overseers. Be shepherds of the assembly of Alahim, which He purchased with His Own blood.
I know that after my departure, savage wolves w ill come in among you and will not
spare the flock. Even from your own number,

men will rise up and distort the truth to draw away disciples after them."

Malaki 4:1-6:
"For look, the yom shall come, burning like a furnace, and all the proud, and every lawless ones shall be stubble. And the yom that shall come shall burn them up," said Yahuah Tsabauth, "which leaves to them neither root nor branch. But to you who fear My Name the Servant of Obedience shall arise with healing in His wings. And you shall go out and leap for joy like calves from the stall. And you shall trample the lawless oness, for they shall be ashes under the soles of your feet on the yom that I do this," said Yahuah Tsabauth.
"Remember the Turah of Mushah, My servant, which I commanded him in Koreb for all Yisharal – laws and directives. See, I am sending you Aliyah the Prophet before the coming of the great and awesome yom of Yahuah. And he shall turn the hearts of the fathers to the children, and the hearts of the children to their fathers, lest I come and smite the arets with utter destruction."

O FOOLISH GALATIONS!

Paul's letter to the Galatians describes the "law" of adult circumcision formerly required for converts to graft into the body, but now that outward sign is done by immersion, calling on the Name of Yahusha for forgiveness. We cannot ask for forgiveness, then turn-away and continue breaking the Ten Commandments. The "law" Paul was referring to was not the Ten Commandments, it was the hand-written law **beside** the ark.

The old covenant was hand-written on a parchment and placed beside the ark (see Dt. 31:26, Heb. 8:13). It was for the offering of animal blood as temporary atonement, now obsolete because Yahusha's blood redeems us completely.

His blood does not allow us to go on sinning. The Ten Commandments are the eternal Covenant, but thought of as obsolete by today's teachers. Paul's writings have been twisted by the untaught, who equivocate his words through casuistry.

http://www.fossilizedcustoms.com/casuistry.html

The tithe is the loudest noise coming out of the steeples, yet it concerns the old covenant. It was food, not money, to support the priesthood and to offer animal blood. The storehouse for that food, the priesthood, and the Temple are not in operation. Don't let anyone bewitch you with men's philosophies, walk as Yahusha walked.

Covenant of Love: A Life & Death Perspective

Heaven and Earth were called as witnesses to the permanence of the Covenant of Love (Dt. 30:19). Only if Heaven and Earth disappear will the Covenant of Love disappear (Mt. 24:35-36 and YirmeYahu 31:35-37). The only change Yahusha made concerned the offering of animal blood by the old priesthood. We now trust in the redemptive blood by which the Ruach ha Qodesh purchased us (Acts 20:28, Dt. 31:28, Hebrews 8:13). The old priesthood and animal blood no longer cover for us, we trust in the blood of Yahusha, our High Priest of the original order of Melkitsedeq.

The shed blood of Yahusha is how our past and future unintentional crimes are now covered, eliminating the former covenant requiring animal blood and the old priesthood.

However without repentance, we can only expect another outcome:

"If we deliberately go on on sinning after we have received the knowledge of the truth, no further offering for sins remains, but only a fearful expectation of judgment and of raging fire that will consume all adversaries." - Hebrews 10:26-27

Teachers have hidden the Name.
Mankind is trained to use very strange words, like GOD, LORD, HASHEM, ADONAI, etc., as if they are names.

Now that we know the real Name of our Deliverer, Provider, Helper, Teacher, and Healer, we must go with what is true, and leave the errors of the past behind.

IESV is a Catholic christogram underlined in the Latin Vulgate, and carried into the Anglican Catholic KJV, still underlined in the first edition.

The underline (bar), or titulos, is a symbol used to indicate the word represents a title that refers to a deity, but the actual name has been encrypted. This was the policy among pagans, who concealed the names of their deities. Yahusha has one Name, and it's Hebrew: yod-hay-uau-shin-ayin (first use seen at Numbers 13:16, check online interlinears). The shin-ayin is a suffix meaning "Deliverer." YAHU + SHA is the transliteration of His Name.

More research here:
http://www.fossilizedcustoms.com/transliteration.html

Deductive Reasoning

A 3rd grader was forced to remove a "Jesus love me" mask by her school. The things people become obsessed about are so ludicrous.
The phrase "JESUS loves me," or "Nimrod loves me," or "Santa Claus loves me" should be viewed as personal opinions at best. The real Name of the messiah is YAHUSHA, not JESUS. JESUS is a name made up as recently as the 16th century. YAHUSHA came in His Father's Name, YAHUAH. Read the Preface of most translations and find the admission that the translators replaced the Name of YAHUAH with the letters LORD (from aduni, kyrios, dominus, which are not even names).

This is a response I posted on a Newsmax TV video found here:
https://youtu.be/d1zbh3i4mXA
Odds are they would not have said anything if the little girl's mask read, *"Muhammad loves me."*

Falsely Called Wisdom

The word *apochryphal* refers to writings that are of doubtful authenticity or authorship. They exhibit anachronisms and geographical errors. Because they are not trustworthy, and translated by Christian theologians who desire to teach their agendas *(and have no idea what they are talking about)* I do not promote the apochryphal books to enhance our mission to teach the Name and Torah. The first Natsarim mentioned Kanok (Enoch), and took the opportunity to warn us about divisions. The first followers of Yahusha did not emphasize the study of the spurious writings which are confusing people today. They warned us about the **divisions** that will ensue in the last days.

Note this comment on an apocalyptic book from Wikipedia:

*"2 Esdras (also called 4 Esdras, Latin Esdras, or Latin Ezra) is the name of an **apocalyptic book** in many English versions of the Bible. Its authorship is ascribed to Ezra, a scribe and priest of the 5th century BCE, although modern scholarship places its composition between 70 and 218 CE."*

1 Timothy 1:1-7: **"Paul, an emissary of Yahusha Mashiak, according to a command of Yahuah our Deliverer, and of Aduni Yahusha Mashiak, our expectation, to Timothy, a genuine child in the belief: Favor, compassion, peace from Yahuah our Father and Yahusha Mashiak our Aduni. As I appealed to you when I went into Makedonia, to remain in Ephesos, in order to command some not to teach differently, nor to pay attention to fables and endless genealogies, which cause disputes rather than an administration of Yahuah which is in belief. Now the goal of this command is love from a clean heart, from a good conscience and a sincere belief, which some, having missed the goal, turned aside to senseless talk, wishing to be teachers of Turah, understanding neither what they say nor concerning what they strongly affirm."**

BIBLE, BIBLICAL - Words Not Found

Danial 10:21 calls the written Word KATHAB
AMATH, writing of truth, not BIBLE.
How can they call on the Name of Yahusha unless
someone is sent to speak it to them?
***"What is highly thought of among men is an
abomination in the sight of Alahim."***
(see Luke 16:14-15)
The guyim will come from the ends of the Earth in
the last days saying, ***"Our fathers have inherited
nothing but futility and lies!"*** YirmeYahu 16:19
The term BIBLE is derived from a fertility deity
giving the ancient city of BYBLOS its name.
The temple of BYBLIA was there.
The coastal city was known for exporting writing
materials made with flax, and so the Greeks used
the deity's name to refer to any book made with flax.
Exodus (Shemoth) 23:13 and Ps. 16:4 tell us not to
take their names on our lips.
Someone recently asked, "what difference does it
make as long as we believe the Bible is the Word of
Truth?"
I would say this in response: Yahuah's Word should
not be referred to by the name of a pagan diety.
Either the Truth takes root, or it is rejected and
eaten by birds. We should tremble at Yahuah's
Word and live in obedience to it. If we are His bride,
we should know what He wants. The difference is
mostly in the perspective we take; either we see
things from our perspective, or Yahusha's.
He says He is a jealous Alahim and wants us to
avoid the polluted customs that have tainted us.
ZefanYah (Zephaniah) 3:9 says He will *purify the
lips / languages of the nations so they will call*
(pronounce, utter) *the Name of Yahuah*. His Name
is Hebrew, and He has one Name. His Name as our

Deliverer is Yahusha, which we call on in the waters of our immersion as we place our trust in His redemption. Some say, "He knows my heart," and they are very correct, because if they have heard the Truth, and reject it in preference to what they have been taught, the leaven in their hearts will remain. He gives us a new wineskin and fills it with new wine, and the old wine has to be rejected.
The *renewing of our minds* is performed by Him, the *Living Word*. Using the names of pagan dieties after learning they are, is rebellious behavior.

How To Handle "Enoch"
It's best to avoid divisions and those who engage in useless arguments (2 Timothy 2:16, 2:23, Romans 16:17, Titus 3:9, Galatians 5:15).
The apochryphal books have unique problems, but the most important one is their prominence. When, where, and who are serious concerns. Yahudah and Kefa (Jude and Peter) quote from the actual words of Kanok, and call him a prophet. The Christian translations of the apochryphal books have anachronistic problems, and terms as well. Because of all the divisiveness the apochryphal books are causing, I'm content with what we read about Kanok's writings from Yahudah (Jude 1:14) and Kefa (2 Peter 1:21). These two first followers of Yahusha confirm that this pre-Deluge obedient-one existed, and both warn us of those who cause divisions among the followers of Yahusha in the last days.
The main point about Kanok in the Natsarim Writings is overlooked, and they argue over how many days are in a pre-Deluge year. Barashith / Genesis 5:24 distinguishes Kanok as exceptionally

obedient, and his life contrasts with the catastrophic end of those who are disobedient.

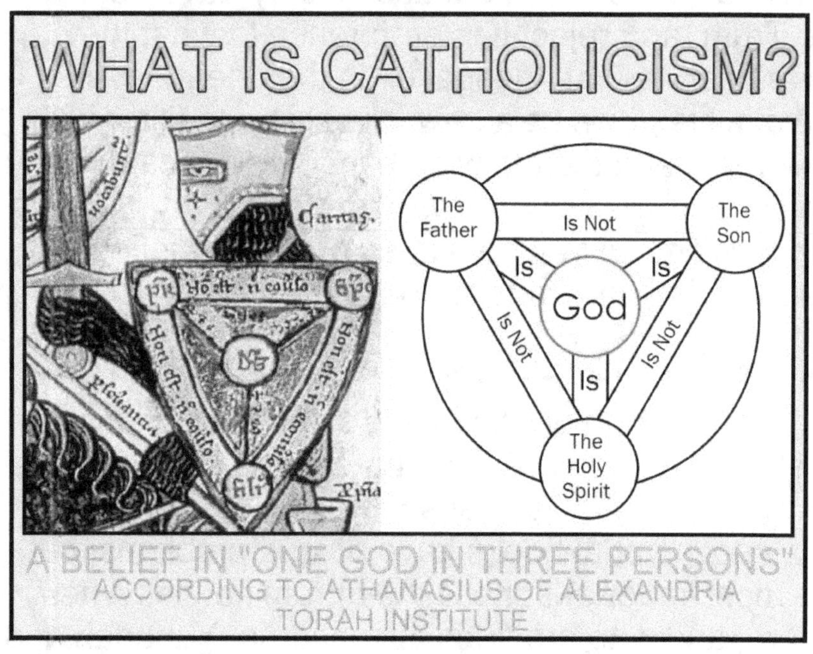

Identity Confusion Of The Third Kind

Catholicism reveres a teacher from Alexandria, Egypt named Athanasius to be the *father of orthodoxy*. Orthodoxy literally means *upright teaching.* Natsarim believe the Father of upright teaching to be the Ruach ha Qodesh.

At the age of 27, Athanasius attended the infamous Nicene Council called by Constantine in 325 CE. His dissertation made *trinitarianism* the prevailing teaching, defeating the *oneness* teaching of Arius. Arius was labelled a heretic afterward.

The writings of Athanasius define Catholicism to be founded on *"the belief in one GOD in 3 persons."* This phrase was incorporated into the Roman Catholics' *Nicene Creed*, due to the persuasion of the 27-year-old Athanasius of Alexandria in 325 CE.

The best explanation of Yahusha's identity is His claim to be the Alef-Tau, and Al Shaddai (Rev. 1:8). Luke 10:22 says only Yahusha reveals the knowledge to an individual. The leaven of men's teachings confuse us with Hinduism's trinities (creator-preserver-destroyer, Brahma-Uishnu-Shiba). We believe Yahuah is One; even demons believe this, and tremble.
http://www.fossilizedcustoms.com/trinity.html
Philip asked Yahusha to show them the Father (Yn. 14), and Yahusha told him ***"He who has seen Me has seen the Father."***

Definition Of Constantine's Christianity
"Her priests have done violence to My Torah and they profane My qodesh things. They have not distinguished between the qodesh and profane, nor

have they made known the difference between the unclean and the clean. And they have hidden their eyes from My Shabathuth, and I am profaned in their midst. Her leaders in her midst are like wolves tearing the prey, to shed blood, to destroy lives, and to get greedy gain. And her prophets have coated them with whitewash, seeing a malicious vision, and divining a lie for them, saying, 'Thus said Aduni Yahuah,' when Yahuah had not spoken. The people of the land extort with extortion, and caused oppression, and committed robbery, and have oppressed the poor and needy. And they oppressed the stranger without lawfulness. And I sought for a man among them who would make a wall, and stand in the break before Me on behalf of the land, that I should not destroy it – but I did not find one! Therefore I have poured out My displeasure on them, I have consumed them with the fire of My wrath. And I have put their way on their own head,' says Aduni Yahuah." (Yekezqal / Ezekiel 22:25-31) The man who outlawed the Shabath day:

The Trinity Controversy
An article worth sharing with you features a good answer to an important question. It is quoted (with parenthetical corrections of terms):
From GotQuestions.org
Article Title: **Why Did Calvin Have Michael Servetus Burned At The Stake For Heresy?**
[begin quote]
"In his denial of the Trinity, Servetus was seen as a heretic by Catholics and Protestants alike. John Calvin briefly corresponded with Servetus, but broke off all communication after the first few letters, as it was apparent that Servetus was unyielding in his

denial of the Trinity.

In 1552 the Spanish Inquisition took action against Servetus, but he escaped their hands. Later, the French Inquisition declared Servetus worthy of death but had to burn him in effigy, due to his escape. In August 1553, Servetus traveled to Geneva where he was recognized and at Calvin's request was imprisoned by the city magistrates. The trial of Michael Servetus lasted through October, at which time the Council of Geneva condemned him to death. Servetus was burned at the stake on October 27, 1553. The Calvinists and the Catholics both wanted him dead, but the Calvinists got to him first.

The condemnation and death of Michael Servetus has been a black mark on John Calvin's record for centuries. Was the burning of Servetus justified, or was it cold-blooded murder? (Alahim) will judge. In contemplating the history of Calvin and Servetus, it is good to remember the following facts:

– The laws in Switzerland made heresy punishable by death; Servetus' death was thus justified in the eyes of the Geneva Council. Plus, the councils of Berne, Zurich, Basle, and Schaffhausen were consulted, and they all encouraged the verdict and punishment.

– Calvin agreed with the sentence of death passed on Servetus; however, he urged that in mercy Servetus be executed by the sword, not by burning. The council rejected his suggestion.

— Michael Servetus was the only heretic ever executed in Geneva in Calvin's lifetime. In comparison, between 3,000 and 10,000 people were executed by Catholics in Spain alone during the Inquisition." [end quote]

The MAGISTERIUM

The Latin word *Magisterium* means "teaching authority." The Greek equivalent to it is *Didascalia*. The *Catachetical School at Alexandria* was the dragon's nest for developing the circus fathers, both *Ante-Nicene* and *Post-Nicene* (terms referring to the teachers before and after the Council of Nicaea in 325 CE).

What should we call ourselves?

One need only be Natsarim, and neither a Catholic (Latin, "universal") nor a Christianos (Greek word for the modern word cretin). Yahusha said, ***"I am the Vine, you are the Natsarim"*** (Yn. 15:5). Paul was accused of being a ***"ringleader of the sect of the Natsarim"*** - Acts 24:5. The Natsarim cry-out on the hills of Afraim in the last days (see YirmeYahu 31:6), not the Christians or Catholics.

We need no other teaching authority to lead us but the living Yahusha in us, Who guides us into all Truth in obedience to do His Word. Google the words Yahusha, and Natsarim. Yahusha and His first Natsarim were neither Catholic, nor Christianos. Their orders were not received from men, but directly from Yahusha, Who breathed on them to understand the Writings of Truth. Men invented the sacraments many centuries after the first Natsarim, and those who set up the Magisterium called us heretics for not recognizing their authority. They chased us into the valleys (labeling us Waldenses), and we were labeled Huguenots in the Jesuit Oath. The dragon is enraged at the offspring of the woman, and makes war against those who obey the Commandments of Alahim, and hold to the testimony of Yahusha - Rev. 12:17.

Yahusha said this to describe His true followers, **"So Yahusha said to those Yahudim who believed Him, 'If you stay in My Word, you are truly My pupils, and you shall know the Truth, and the Truth shall make you free.'"** -Yn. 8:31-32

Identify A Tree By Its Fruit
Yahuah manifested Himself in these last days as the Son (Hebrews 1:1-3, Acts 20:28), and gave Himself to purchase us. Yahuah is One Alahim, and there is no other deliverer besides Him. We identify an evil tree by the fruit it bears. From Constantine to the Inquisition, and from the Jesuit oath to the United Nations and its initiatives, the controller has tightened his grip over mankind progressively. He knows his time is short.

The Trinity Stronghold (youtube video)
A method called eisegesis (taking what is already believed to a study from outside) has persuaded (or seduced) people to believe an ancient error inherited from pagan cultures. This video will convince you, not persuade you.
Yahuah is Yahusha, but the trinity (3 persons in one) infection from the Nicene Creed conceals this fact. Constantine was persuaded by Athanasius of Alexandria to impose the trinity doctrine. This made Athanasius inherit the title: "Father of Orthodoxy."
https://youtu.be/8cyGWz_qpgo

Messenger Of The Covenant (Mal. 3:1)
"'See, I am sending My Messenger, and He shall prepare the way before Me. Then suddenly the Master you are seeking comes to His Hekal, even the Messenger of the Covenant, in Whom you delight. See, He is coming!' said Yahuah of armies."
Who can stand when He appears?
Yahusha is alive, and He speaks to us through His body, His Natsarim. Revelation 19:10 tells us the testimony of Yahusha is the Spirit of prophecy. YashaYahu 42:8 & 43:11 helps us overcome the twinitarian and trinitarian tendencies inherited from the circus. Yahusha's omnipresence (being in all places and all His people at the same time) helps us realize Who He is, but ultimately only He can reveal this to an individual, as He told us at Luke 10:22. The Ruach ha Qodesh shed His blood to purchase us (Acts 20:28). To do this, Yahuah manifested Himself in human form (Hebrews 1:1-3). Arius was correct; Athanasius and the Nicene Creed are incorrect.

Spiritual Bullying Happens
When we see condemnation and dissensions, we are not seeing the fruits of Yahusha, but rather the works of the flesh (Galatians 5).
The interpretation of prophecy, factions, and calendar issues will only continue to fragment into more and more divisions over time.
No codes, skin, hidden knowledge, or calendar ever redeemed anyone, but the redemptive appointments are outlines (shadows) of what

Yahusha has, and is doing to manifest His love and redemptive power (Dt. 16, Lev. 23).

It is no longer we who live; but Mashiak lives in us. Many walk among us as teachers, but they do not yet belong to Him. By their fruits, you will identify them.

Is Hashem The Redeemer?

Tradition is *leaven*, and blocks us from pure Truth. Guard yourselves and the whole flock from those who distort the Truth.

The message of redemption is to the Yahudi first, and also to the guyim. The Alahim of Abrahim, Yitshaq, and Yaqub is not Hashem, His Name is Yahuah (YashaYahu 42:8). AliYahu dealt with this LORD-GOD thing at Mt. Karmal 1 Kings 18).

Yahuah manifested Himself in many diverse ways in the past, and in these last days He did so in a body we call the Son, Yahusha. Eberim (Hebrews) chapter 1 explains this.

All native and non-native branches of the fig tree rely on the life of the same tree. Should they hate the other branches or feel more entitled?

All Yisharal will be delivered by the Deliverer, and He is One. Yahusha is our kohen ha gadol, everlasting Father, Paraklita (Helper), Counselor, and King. The Ruach ha Qodesh (set-apart Spirit of Yahusha) made some to be overseers of the assembly, and He shed His Own blood to purchase us (Acts 20:28).

In the NAME of GOD?

Who is GOD?

GOD is the word for the *"mighty ones"* of heathen myth. Nimrod, the first king on Earth, built Babel. He was a mighty man, against Yahuah. The Creator of

Heaven and Earth is not one of these might ones, His only Name given is YAHUAH, and He is Yahusha, our only Deliverer. Google YAHUSHA. Learn His Name, and what the mystagogues have hidden from you by their traditions. Our fathers have inherited nothing but lies and futility, and there is no value in any of their traditions.
https://youtu.be/VOYYCkVazBl
Watch **Obsolete Man** (*Twilight Zone*) at the link

Were You Baptized Into A Circus?
A video discussion on being sealed for the day of our redemption, and our pledge of a good conscience by calling on the Name of Yahusha. There is no other name under heaven given among men by which we must be delivered.
If we know all secrets, and gain all understanding, we do not merit a higher status above others in Yahusha's eyes. The meek and humble will inherit the Earth. Translations are interpretations. The one thing that really matters is accepting the blood of Yahusha by immersing in water and calling on His Name for the forgiveness of our crimes. We are truly His talmidim if we abide in His Word and we let Him guide us in doing the things that please Him. Geometry, our skin color, a re-built Temple, finding the Ark of the Covenant, heavenly scrolls, and speaking in tongues can't deliver anyone.

One Blood – Acts 17:26
A one-sentence comment someone left on one of my youtube videos stated,
"White people are not Yahuah's children."

I'm a blend of Yahudi, Cherokee, and other tribes, but certainly we may all claim to be descendants of Adam, the son of Yahuah (Luke 3:38).
Are foreigners lost, or rather are they our mission? Acts 17:26 says all *nations* (H1471 *GUYIM*) were created from one blood.
The house of Yisharal is blended with *all races*, as foretold at Amos 9:9. Yahuah sent Paul to speak to the Greeks (Acts 17:26),
"from one man, Yahuah created all the nations."
The original city-states of Greece were first settled by descendants of the tribe of Dan, and all Hellenists were called Danites by historians.
Danites were the builders of the Trojan horse. "Dan crossed-over" is the meaning of the Danube River.
YashaYahu 56:3-8 says foreigners who join themselves to Yahuah and guard Shabath are welcome.
Uyiqara / Lev. 24:22 Yekezqal / Ez. 47:22 both tell us not to distinguish between the native-born Yisharali and a foreigner. Ruth was obviously a prime example, being included in the lineage of Yahusha Himself.
Miriam and Aharon spoke against the Kushite wife Mushah had taken, and Miriam became leprous over her conversation (Numbers 12). Yahuah does not look upon the outward appearance, but rather on the heart of man. (1 Shemual 16:7). Watch:
http://www.fossilizedcustoms.com/mirror.html
Mt. 28:19 gives us our orders as Natsarim. Teach all nations the Name and to obey everything we were commanded to obey. Blessed are those found doing their orders at His return (Mt. 24:46).

You Are Dust, And To Dust You Will Return

Yahuah made all mankind from one blood (Acts 17:26). He struck Miryam with leprosy for her verbal criticism of the Cushite wife her brother Mushah had taken (Numbers 12). The tribes of Yisharal have been finely scattered among the guyim (Zechariah 10:9, Amus 9:9). Yahuah does not look upon the outward appearance, but on the heart, which is our thinking (1 Shemual 16:7). Philip was used to explain the text of YashaYahu 53 to an Ethiopian eunuch returning to his queen Candace (Acts 8:26-40). All of these texts, and many more, show that the sin of bigotry is very serious. Run from teachers who teach their own superiority, and run to Yahusha. Soon, all races will see His scars, and shut their mouths because they will see and understand what they had never been told (YashaYahu 52:15).

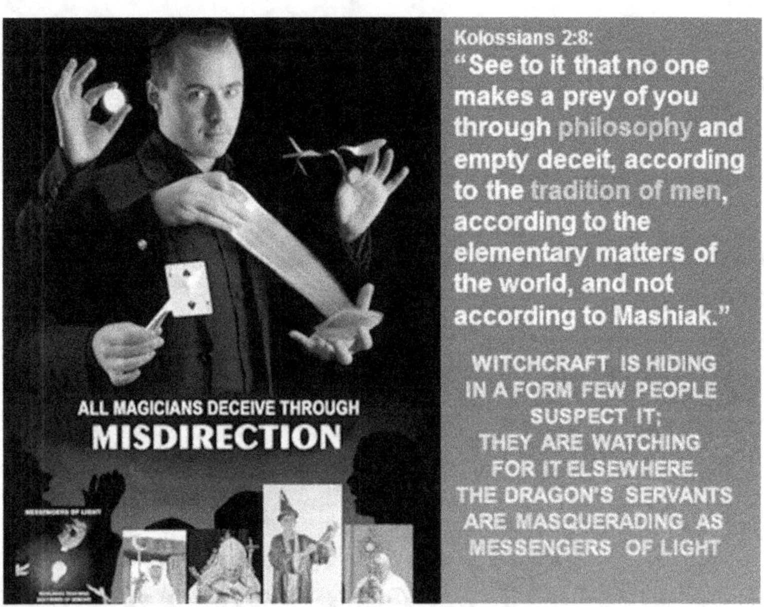

Hebrew Israelite Misdirection

There's a great deal of discussion on the Internet concerning populations claiming to be the original chosen people, and use skin color as a basis. What is most important? The most important day of our life in the flesh is the day we are immersed, calling on the Name of Yahusha, and joining to Him (sealed as His property). This act places a person in Covenant with Yahuah, restoring them to favor because they trust in Yahusha's blood. What does our own bloodline have to do with our redemption? Not too much! Arabs are Hebrews (descendants of Eber), and have remained unmoved from the area they inhabit to this day.

Arabs are Eberim (Hebrews). The children Abrahim produced by the Egyptian girl Hagar & and Keturah after Sarah passed, are cousins of Yitshaq and Yaqub. Yaqub is Abrahim's grandson. Yaqub's descendants are the 12 tribes of "Israel" (Yisharal), and they are also Eberim. Shalomoh (Solomon) dispersed the tribes of Yasharal into the "islands of sea" by making colonies all over the Earth. Unlike the Hebrew Arabs who stayed in their ancient lands for the most part, the *Hebrew Yisharalim* (Israelites) have literally *become* the nations. Yahuah's promise to Abrahim at Barashith / Genesis 15 is restated at Amus 9:9. Abrahim's name means *father of nations*.

Is Celebrating A Birthday Pagan?
What is highly thought of among men is an abomination in the sight of Alahim. - Luke 16:14-15 Celebrating our own, our family members, or Yahusha's birth is an abomination in Yahuah's sight. The 7-day festival we observe in the seventh month (Sukkoth, Tabernacles, Tents) is an outline of several things. Yahusha was born on the first day of Sukkoth, and on the last great day (number 8) He was circumcised. Another picture we have of this

time is the freedom from Farah, and on the 7th day his armies drowned along with him, and the equipment of his army. Thirdly, we look forward to the same period in the future, when we will see the marriage supper of the Lamb, and come under His kuppah, the wedding tent, symbolic of His household.

The warnings and promises are about to kick-in ferociously very soon. Seraphim (burning ones) will be released to reap the Earth, first taking away the disobedient inhabitants, then gathering Yahusha's wheat into His barn, or wedding kuppah.

The world's customs are programmed into each person from birth, and we would not know what a "birthday celebration" is unless we were not trained to know about them. The birthdays celebrated in Scripture stand out - the Farah celebrated his, Herod celebrated his, and the children of Iyob celebrated theirs. Death occurred in each case.

What About Kanukah?
The story / account of Kanukah is found in the record of the Maccabee's (2 Maccabees 4). It records their overthrow of the Greek tyrant Antiochus Epiphanes, and the heinous acts he perpetrated on the Yahudim.
Kanukah (Dedication) is mentioned at Yn. 10:22-23. It's not one of the moedim, but rather a civil celebration much like the celebration of Thanksgiving in the USA, to be thankful for the ending of the civil war. Abraham Lincoln put down a rebellion, and the Maccabees stamped-out the

Hellenization of their culture. Kanukah is a civil celebration, but a very important one - although not commanded. Maccabees is not an apochyphal (spurious) written record, but quite real. It's historical events really happened, and what we can teach future generations about it should be continued.
http://www.fossilizedcustoms.com/hanukkah.html

Who Started Thanksgiving Day?

It was not the Pilgrims, yet most people are taught this in school. Every country has a history of its own. At the end of the U.S. Civil War, Abraham Lincoln instituted a national day of thanks to commemorate the end of that horrible Jesuit-Illuminati division over the Emancipation Proclamation, freeing all human beings from enslavement. The north followed the law, but the southern states did not, wanting to maintain the right to own human beings to work their plantations. The pope wrote letters before and during that war, which contain outrageous evidence of a conspiracy to rebel against the north, divide the United States of America, and addressed his letters to "Mr. President" in Charleston, S.C. Thanksgiving Day was instituted to give thanks to Yahuah for ending the war the Jesuits hoped would destroy the U.S.A. The U.S. Constitution as written would never allow any alliance to make a concordat with the Vatican, and after the war Lincoln was assassinated. 12 Jesuit operatives were hanged for the conspiracy. After this, another ferocious attempt to divide the U.S.A. was formed, also based in Charleston, S.C. It was called the Ku Klux Klan. The attempt to

foment a race war has continued since the 1860's, and Lincoln wrote about this foreign enemy and its conspirators, and he called them Jesuits. They ran all the departments of the Nazis, planning to take over the world. They control the news media, the United Nations, and hide in plain sight as they blame others for their activities. Read the Jesuit Oath, and what is happening in the world today will begin to form a coherent pattern:
http://www.fossilizedcustoms.com/jesuitoath.htm

YOUR WORD, YOUR NAME, ABOVE ALL - PS. 138:2

The branch belongs to the Vine, and the Vine belongs to the Gardener. In the context of the term Branch, Yahusha is the manifestation of Yahuah Himself (See YashaYahu 4:2 & 11:1-4).

The Stone The Builders Rejected

If it falls on you, it will crush you (Mt. 21:42-44). The tradition to not pronounce the Name began during the Babylonian captivity.

It became policy to stone anyone (other than a kohen) that pronounced the Name aloud.

Yahuah is very angry that His Name is not spoken (YirmeYahu 23:27).

From Yahuah's perspective, hiding His Name to protect it from being misused by those who might profane it indicates to Him another kind of strange fire. He never said to hide it for any reason.

YirmeYahu said it was like a fire burning in his bones, and he could not hold it back. As early as YirmeYahu's time, they had caused His Name to be forgotten by not using it. His Name was forgotten for BEL (Baal, meaning LORD). At 1 Kings 18, AliYahu called on Yahuah: prophets of the LORD failed.

Revelation 3:8 gives us more insight:

"I know your deeds. See, I have placed before you an open door that no one can shut. I know that you have little strength, yet you have guarded My Word and have not denied My Name."

At YashaYahu 42:8, Yahuah says:

"I am Yahuah. That is My Name."

Any argument insisting otherwise needs to be taken up with Him.

There is one Alahim, and Yahusha quoted the Shema as the greatest command.

Phillip had not recognized Him as the Father, and then Phillip made the statement, *"My Aduni and my Alahim!"* (Yn. 20:28).

THE GREATEST COMMANDMENT

Yaqub 2 is a warning letter to all generations. In examining that message, we find a statement that contradicts what Christianity has inherited.
Yaqub says,
"You believe that Yahuah is ONE, you do well. Even demons believe, and shudder in terror."
It is a reference to the greatest Commandment often called the SHEMA at Dt. 6:4-9.
Yahusha confirms it as the highest of all instructions at Mt. 22:36-40.
The majority do not recognize that Yahuah is Yahusha in all the confusing clutter of men's doctrines. Constantine's trinitarian creed at Nicaea was formed from the proposal of Athanasius of Alexandria, yet few people know about all the adopted paganism they are surrounded by.

The Black Obelisk of Shalmaneser III is the only portrayal of a king of Israel. Yahu (JEHU) is shown bowing to Shalmaneser III King YAHU is shown wearing a phrygian cap to indicate his enslavement. Free men did not normally wear hats. The Assyrian panel shows the Solar deity Ahura Mazda / Shamash as a winged star, and larger star to the right.

The only known portrayal of an Israelite ruler is on a panel of Shalmaneser's black obelisk. This obelisk is on display at the British Museum in London.
The 10th ruler of the Northern tribes was YAHU (JEHU) son of Omri, and is shown bowing to Shalmaneser III on the black obelisk.

In the ancient world, all male slaves, including freed
slaves, were expected to wear a floppy cap called a
phrygian cap. Free men did not normally wear a hat.
Later, the 70-year captivity to Babel caused
Yahudah to adopt the script of their captors,
Aramaic. Danial was called to read the real Eberith
script on the wall at Belshazzar's last party.
Celebrating the destruction of Jerusalem, the Arch
of Titus shows the menorah of Yahuah's Temple
being hauled away, and the survivors of the city of
Yerushalim enslaved. The Arch of Titus, the Arch of
his father Vaspasian, and the Coliseum were built
with the gold taken from Yahuah's Temple in 70 CE.

Another conqueror's stone, the Moabite Stone at
the Louvre Museum in Paris, shows the Name of
Yahuah in the real Eberith / Hebrew script.

Why Is Yahusha's Name Shortened On The Ossuary Of Yaqub?

The one use of the *hypocorisma* form* at Nekemyah 8:17 shows a diminished spelling for the successor of Mushah: **yod-shin-uau-ayin**.
The other 216 uses of the *full name* are overwhelming: **yod-hay-uau-shin-ayin**.
The origin, or first use of the name is at Numbers (Bamidbar) 13:16, showing the addition of the letter yod to the name Husha (yod + hay-uau-shin-ayin).
The pressure to avoid the utterance of the Name YAHUAH persists, and this is most likely why the inscription reads as it does on the ossuary (bone box announced in 2002) of Yaqub, Yahusha's brother. The inscription is in Aramith script, and translated reads:

"Yaqub ben Yusef brother of Yeshua"
*hypocorisma - a diminished form of a name is seen on the ossuary of Yaqub.

Other contexts with same spelling

The word meaning "deliver" or "salvation" in 28 other contexts is not a name, but the same spelling as the hypocorisma (diminutive form) at NekemYah 8:17. The other 28 occurrences do not refer to the son of Nun, who was originally HUSHA (hay-uau-shin-ayin), and re-named by Mushah by the addition of one letter, yod. His new name became YAHUSHA (yod-hay-uau-shin-ayin, see Numbers 13:16).

In these other 28 cases, the yod-shin-uau-ayin are translated in sentences as nouns conveying the meaning of salvation, welfare, or prosperity. Interlinear examples will show this, such as YashaYahu 26:1 where it is expressed in the feminine gender form. Whether short, long, feminine gender, prefix, suffix, or a proper name, all share the root YASHA (yod-shin-ayin), the first letters in the Name YASHAYAHU (spelled yod-shin-ayin-yod-hay-uau). ALISHA (ALI+SHA in Hebrew spelled alef-lamed-yod-shin-ayin) uses the same suffix SHA seen in the Name YAHUSHA. As people learn to define words and names from the context of the words, fewer controversies will persist as they have.

Passover vs. Communion

Passover is a night to be remembered throughout our generations.

We observe the memorial of Yahusha's death on the night He ate matsah and drank wine with His first Natsarim. At Mt. 26:29 He told them He would not drink of the fruit of the vine again "until I drink it anew with you in My Father's reign."

Matsah is part of the remembrance meal, reminding us of Yahusha's body being given by Him, and shared with His followers.

They asked where to **"observe the Passover,"** now known as the remembrance of Yahusha's death. He called the red wine the cup of the renewed Covenant in His blood, remembering it was shed to remit the sins of the world.

The observance is always done in private homes, just as the first Passover in Egypt.

Yahusha is our Passover. Catholicism calls their bread ritual "receiving communion," ignoring the remembrance of Yahusha's death at the proper time once each year. Paul told us to guard / keep / observe the feast without leaven at 1 Korinthians 5:7.

He mentioned that Yahusha is our Passover, and to observe the appointment with pure hearts, without the leaven of immoral people when we remember this night our Deliverer atoned for the sins of the world.

Let's Keep It Simple

Yahusha renewed the covenant that He found fault with, and replaced it with a permanent solution. The instructions to temporarily atone for sin were written on a scroll and placed beside the ark (Dt. 31:26), requiring animal blood offered by the old priesthood. That was eliminated by the permanent solution: Yahusha's blood shed for all unintentional sin. The change in priesthood and the decrees to atone for sin are obsolete, and Hebrews 8:13 discusses this change. The renewed, or altering of the agreement, was predicted at YirmeYahu 31:31. It has been accomplished by the one offering of Yahusha's blood, and He circumcises the hearts of all that turn away from sin, accept His blood as the offering for sin, and He writes His Commandments on their hearts. He renews us with His life, and we walk as He walked. Those who control teachings have added and taken away from the Living Word.

Natsarim guard and teach the Commandments, and do so as commissioned by Yahusha. We would not call our precious Yahusha* by man-made names or titles, or deny His Name in any way. That controversy was settled at Mt. Karmal; AliYahu against the priests of BEL and ASHERAH. All the people shouted, ***"Yahuah - He is Alahim!"***
*Yahuah has become our Deliverer: Yahuah is Yahusha ha Mashiak. There is no other deliverer, nor any other Rock. His Name is the Stone the builders rejected.

Preterism, Dispensationalism, Replacement Theology, & The Beast

Fallacies surely exist because no one is infallable, except Yahusha. Prophecies have sometimes been shown to have multiple fulfillments. Preterism is highly fallable as a method of interpretation, holding that many prophecies concerning the end of days have already been fulfilled. Malaki 4:1-6, Danial 7:25, and Danial 12 reveal insights about the extreme last days that most inhabitants of the Earth have been vaccinated against with replacement theology and dispensationalism. The weeds will be taken out first, burned, and the wheat gathered into the barn regardless of men's understanding about the order of events. The wrath of Yahuah will be poured-out on the *disobedient* inhabitants of the Earth, and those who misled them will receive a much more severe judgment. Yahuah does not change, but the teaching authorities of the beast paint a different picture, poisoning the expectations of most people.

What is the beast? It's the World Order, also known as the reign of Babel. It's organized in three echelons of authority:

Clergy-Nobility-Laity, the principalities, or estates, of world power.

http://www.fossilizedcustoms.com/beast.html

Tongues & Languages vs. Ears & Hearing

The manifestations of *tongues* we normally see today among Pentecostals are viewed as a sign of receiving the gift of languages from the Spirit of Yahusha. This is not the way to understand the prophecy of YashaYahu / Isa-iah 28:11, because the verse must be understood from the whole of chapter 28. Today's thinking about *tongues* as a gift to the body of Yahusha was not the confusion manifested at the tower of Babel, but rather it was a gift of *hearing*. It was given to the assembly so the diverse people gathered together could *hear* the message of deliverance in their own language. As long as there are people who continue to speak in diverse languages, and have ears to hear, the prophecy continues to unfold everywhere. The English language has galloped and exploded into the whole world as a convergence of the Age of Colonization, the printing press, and the Anglican Catholic KJV. English has become the dominant *jabbering lip* Yahuah is continuing to use to speak to His people that He scattered into the nations. Those who have ears to hear His call to turn back to Him are the ones being sealed in their foreheads, and call on the Name Yahusha. Watch a video about the KJV: https://youtu.be/Ec2EliKxnD8

What Is His Name, And What Is His Son's Name?

No one should believe in JESUS, it's an invented word and not even 500 years old.

What's His Real Name? It's found at least 216 times in the TaNaK, and it's based on the Tetragrammaton, and first seen at Numbers 13:16: YAHUSHA (I am your Deliverer).

Looking at the Los Lunas Stone in NM, USA, one immediately sees how the script we carried back from our captors (Aramith) altered the Eberith script & tongue. Almost 400 years before Danial and the rest of Yahudah were taken away to Babel Land, Shalomoh sent ships to remote areas of the Earth, resulting in settled colonies where they left way-marks of their presence. The descendants of those colonies remain among several tribes who speak the Name "YAHUAH" - one of them is the Cherokee (indigenous tribe in North America). Their Name for the "great spirit" is uttered with all vowels, exactly as Clement rendered the transliteration in Greek letters, IAOUE. Yusef Ben MatithYahu (Flavius Josephus) saw the Eberith script on the headpiece of the kohen ha gadol, and the Name written in four vowels. He did not see it written in the script of our captors, Aramith; he called it "Eberith" (that is, Hebrew in today's vernacular). The DSS contain no vowel marks; the letters themselves are enough to pronounce the language. The niqqud marks appeared in the 8th century CE, and are best ignored. YashaYahu 9:16: "For those who guide this people are leading them astray; and those who are guided by them are brought into confusion."

What is the Pearl of Great Price?
The Name of Yahuah, Creator of Heaven & Earth, is the *Pearl of Great Price*, like a *treasure hidden in a field* (the world). A video discussion on a stone etched with the Ten Commandments emphasizes

how significant the Name of Yahusha is (this link is active in the eBook): https://lnkd.in/ew6ivMY Physical evidence of the Hebrew Name is inscribed on a gatestone estimated to be 10th century BCE, during the colonization period of King Solomon.

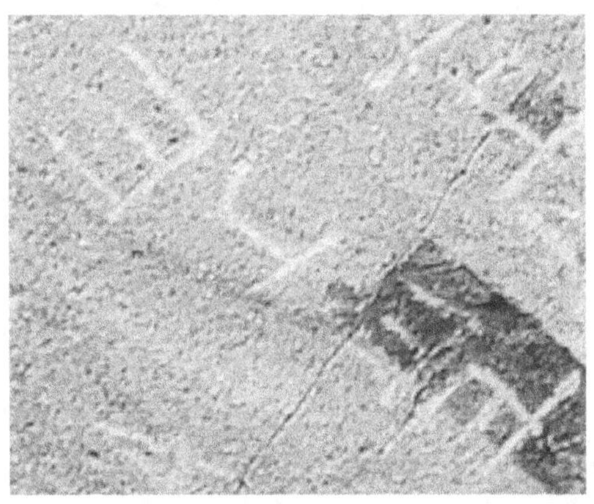

Natsarim only trust in Yahusha for Truth because He purchased us with His own blood (Acts 20:28). At Yn. 5:43, Yahusha said He came in His Father's Name, and they would not receive Him. If another comes in another name, like HESUS or IESU, him they will receive. Acts 4:12 tells us there is one Name, and finding it buried by the world's languages is like a priceless pearl. It's Hebrew. Names are not translated to use as what they mean, but names are called on as they are given in their original language.
The Name above all names is no longer whispered in secret, it's being shouted from the rooftops. This is happening now (Mt. 23:39).

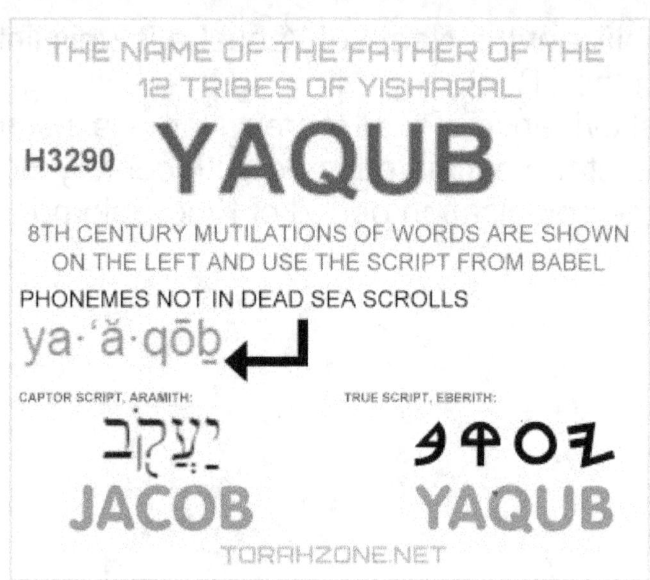

YAQUB: Father of the 12 Tribes

The brother from another mother (Arabs, also being Hebrews / Eberim) name their children with a closer phonology to the original. Yaqub and Yusef are common male names. They have not corrupted their speech with niqqud vowels invented in the 8th century as happened to the Yahudim. The Arabs have preserved the sounds of the language very well, and they have never been exiled from their lands. The influences of Hinduism when India swelled its borders around 200 BCE brought cultural changes, but not to their speech. Radical acceptance of Truth is difficult at first, but those who guide / control teachings lead many into confusion, and this is an example of what was done to the language of Eber.

Yahuah became our Deliverer, Yahusha.

The suffix (SHA) uses the shin-ayin to mean "deliverer" from the root, YASHA.
(see also the name *YashaYahu*, aka "Isaiah").

The spelling yod-hay-uau-hay (Yahuah) is used in
the TaNaK 6823 times in the Eberith Scriptures.
Interlinear translations will verify the following:
Mushah (Moses) added the letter yod to his
assistant's name: Y + HUSHA see Num. 13:16
Three spellings are found in the TaNaK for the
same name given to our Mashiak:
1 time: yod-shin-uau-ayin (hypocorisma or
diminutive form, YSHUA) see NekemYah 8:17
2 times: yod-hay-uau-shin-uau-ayin (YAHUSHUA)
The two uses of this 6-lettered spelling are found at
Deut. 3:21 and Judges. 2:7.
216 times: yod-hay-uau-shin-ayin (YAHUSHA) see
ZekarYah 3

HYKSOS HOAX

The predominant spelling is best to teach and use,
since it is the one most likely devoid of scribal errors
or directed attacks on Yahuah's Name written most
often in the Scriptures of Truth. Close examination
of the charts shown around the Internet combine
real Eberith pictographic script with Hieroglyphic
pictographs. The Hieroglyphic letters are not
Eberith, and no physical evidence of them being
used by Yisharal to write anything, and certainly not
the Name, has ever been discovered.

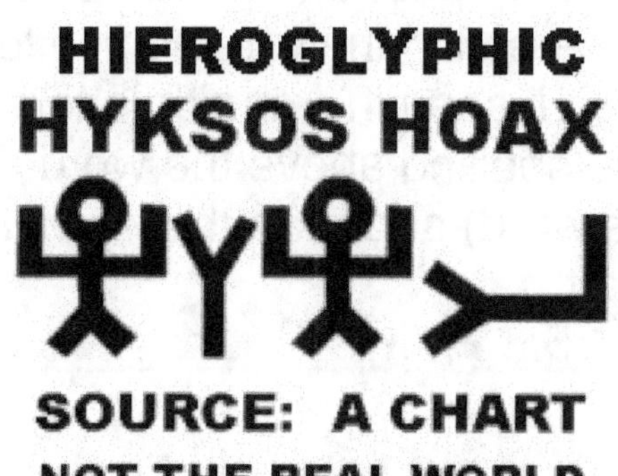

Hieroglyphics is not a script used by the prophets in any of the writings, but has become very important to teachers on the Internet. As for the meaning of the suffix, shin-ayin (SHA), teachers differ in the contextual meaning of it, which is easily corrected when we study. It comes from the same root seen in the names Alisha (Elisha) and YashaYahu (Isaiah): YASHA (yod-shin-ayin). Shua means cry out, but when Mushah invented the word YAHUSHA, he only added a yod to what already existed, hay-uau-shin-ayin, *HUSHA*. There is not a SHUA (shin-uau-ayin) in the name HUSHA, although after the Masoretes added their uninspired vowels to the word, it came to be JOSHUA in all the references following the KJV. Transliterating with babbling languages which were mutilated by foreign lips before we were born isn't easy to overcome.

Use Eberith Sources, Not Greek Or Latin
The Latin letters we use on the Internet attempt to imitate the sounds of the *Eberith* letters. In the Scripture of Truth we find five letters used 216 times in this arrangement: **yod-hay-uau-shin-ayin.**
The last two letters are a suffix, shin-ayin, used in another name: ALISHA. The various spellings, niqqud marks, and apostrophes can be dispensed with when we carefully analyze the five letters in an interlinear, even if seen in Aramith letters. At the link, look at the spelling above the word **JOSHUA** (an inaccurate word) and read the *Aramith* lettering from right-to-left:
https://biblehub.com/interlinear/zechariah/3.htm

What do you see from this evidence, and which
transliteration is arranged best from these popular
spellings:
YESHUA?
YAHSHUA?
YAHUSHUA?
YAHUSHA?
IESV, IHS, IESOUS, and JESUS are impossible
once you see the evidence, and the arrangements
of the five letters shown in the Interlinear eliminates
the first 3 in the above list. Don't just be persuaded;
be convinced.
Study; but please avoid disputing with those who
reject the physical evidence.

Natsarim only trust in Yahusha for Truth because He
purchased us with His own blood (Acts 20:28).
At Yn. 5:43, Yahusha said He came in His Father's
Name, and they would not receive Him. If another
comes in another name, like HESUS or IESU, him
they will receive. Acts 4:12 tells us there is one
Name, and finding it buried by the world's
languages is like a priceless pearl. It's Hebrew.
**Names are not translated to use as what they
mean, but they are called on as they sound in
their original language.** The Name above all
names is no longer whispered in secret, it's being
shouted from the rooftops. This is happening now
(Mt. 23:39).

The **BYNV** uses the transliteration (not translation)
of the Hebrew letters, yod-hay-uau-shin-ayin:
YAHU+SHA. The transliteration ALISHA is
produced from alef-lamed-yod-shin-ayin.
YASHAYAHU is produced from yod-shin-ayin+yod-

hay-uau. The (+) I've added for emphasis, as Hebrew often uses a prefix or suffix to modify the root. We use Latin letters to produce the sounds of foreign words.

The YEHO spelling is inaccurate, since it reflects the effects of the 8th century meddling of the Masoretes (a Karaite sect) who added "niqqud marks" to divert the proper utterance. They molested the texts to cue a reader to say "ADUNI" in place of the four-vowels of the Name, yod-hay-uau-hay, "YAHUAH." Names and places are transliterated to produce the identical sound phonetically, but to translate a word produces the meaning of a word. Many names beginning with the letter alef (A) have been traditionally turned into other transliterations for example,

ALIYAHU became "ELIJAH," ALISHA became "ELISHA," and YAHUSHA became "JOSHUA."

Investigate For Yourself

Acts 4:12 grabbed my thoughts the first time I read it. The jeopardy a person is in for denying the Name is sin, so I have to tell you.

In the event that some don't yet know Who YAHUSHA is, the translators purged the real Name of our Creator.

The KJV (an Anglican Catholic version of the Latin Vulgate) inserted a "device" (IESV) to replace the real Name. Now it's everywhere.

We are using Latin letters to write our "English" words here. Our numbers are Arabic, and thankfully not Roman numerals, which also use Latin letters to represent quantities. To break the spell of many misunderstandings, everyone should research the Name, YAHUSHA.

Yahuah is Yahusha. Hebrews 1:1-3 & Acts 20:28 reveals to us Who He is. Belief is dead without obedience, and only Yahusha's indwelling can make that happen.

Did You Know? Yahusha Is Omnipresent!
Yahusha is Yahuah, and every knee in heaven and on Earth will bow, and every tongue will admit this when He appears again. Yahusha is the Name Yahuah with the added suffix SHA (Deliverer). It's the only (Eberith / Hebrew) Name given among men to call on for the forgiveness of their sins against the eternal Covenant. Other names used to encrypt this Name have been used in Greek and Latin translations such as IESOUS, IHS, IESU, IC-XC, and as recently as the 17th century the term JESUS became the most widely known form.
Yahusha raised Himself from the dead, and said so at Yn. 2:19. He told Philip the one who sees Him has seen the Father (Yn. 15:9). Hebrews 1:1-3 leaves no doubt, but for those who do, we have Rev. 1:8 where He declares He is Al Shaddai. "My son, Alahim will provide Himself a Lamb . . ." (Barashith 22:8, also see Mt. 11:27, and YashaYahu 43:11 which states there is no deliverer besides Yahuah).
Yahusha is omnipresent, which no other being in the universe can be, unless that being is the Alahim who made all things. All things seen and unseen were CREATED by, and for, Yahusha (Kolossians 1:16). There is a difference between *making stuff* (forming stuff from other stuff), and *creating stuff*. Yahusha created all other beings, and one day all the ruachim (spirits) will worship Him, as most already do.

When Philip asked to see the Father, Yahusha said something amazing.
Scripture tells us that no one knows the Son except the Father, and no one knows the Father except the Son, and who the Son chooses to reveal (Mt. 11:27).
At Yn. 14:9, Yahusha asked Philip how he could ask to see the Father, having been with him so long. Then He said that he that has seen Him has seen the Father. Philip knelt down to say "my Aduni and my Alahim!" Yahusha never told Philip to get up and worship only the Father. Acts 20 tells us the Ruach ha Qodesh shed His Own blood to purchase us.
The greatest Torah instruction is Hear Yisharal; Yahuah is our Alahim; Yahuah is One, affirmed by Yahusha at Mark 12:29 (from Dt. 6:4). Demons also belief He is One, and tremble.
Yahuah is Yahusha ha Mashiak, but few know this Truth. Yahusha's Name means "I am your Deliverer."
There is no other Deliverer, except Yahuah (YashaYahu 42).
He will not give His praise to another.
See also Hebrews / Eberim 1:1-3

Is Santa Fact, Or Fiction?
This fact about the father of lies is coming out more and more, and Nimrod's Secret Identity as the first human to be worshiped as a Solar deity explains why offerings are left for Him in homes when he comes out of the FIRE place. Cookies, milk, or donuts (food offerings) are placed before the gohonzon altar in the homes of those who come from the actual land of Nimrod. One of my books is

titled Nimrod's Secret Identity, The Greatest Conspiracy On Earth.

Breaking News: SATAN is unmasked from his Nimrod disguise. Stop lying to your children about the solar deity posing as an angel of light:

https://youtu.be/1U1Ed2z2t-w

EXODUS / SHEMOTH 20:2-17

Google: **BYNV** torahzone.net

I AM YAHUAH ALAHIM-OF YOU WHO BROUGHT YOU OUT FROM LAND OF MITSRAYIM FROM HOUSE OF

SLAVERIES. NOT HE SHALL BE TO YOU ALAHIM OTHER ONES BEFORE FACE OF ME

NOT YOU MAKE FOR SELF IDOL OR ANY IMAGE THAT IN SKIES FROM ABOVE OR THAT

ON ARETS FROM BENEATH OR THAT IN WATERS FROM BENEATH TO ARETS NOT YOU BOW

TO THEM AND NOT YOU WORSHIP THEM FOR I AM YAHUAH AL OF YOU AL JEALOUS. PUNISHING

SIN OF FATHERS ON CHILDREN TO THIRDS AND TO FOURTH TO ONES HATING ME BUT SHOWING LOVE

O THOUSANDS TO ONES LOVING ME AND TO ONES GUARDING OF COMMANDS OF ME. NOT YOU TAKE NAME YAHUAH

ALAHIM OF YOU FOR RUIN FOR NOT HE HOLD GUILTLESS YAHUAH WHO TAKES NAME OF HIM

FOR RUIN. TO REMEMBER DAY OF THE SHABATH TO SEPARATE; SIX OF DAYS YOU SHALL LABOR

AND YOU SHALL DO ALL OF WORK OF YOU BUT DAY OF THE SEVENTH IS SHABATH TO YAHUAH ALAHIM OF YOU

NOT YOU DO ANY OF WORK YOU OR SON OF YOU OR DAUGHTER OF YOU MANSERVANT OF YOU

OR MAIDSERVANT OF YOU OR ANIMAL OF YOU OR ALIEN OF YOU WHO WITHIN GATES OF YOU

FOR SIX OF DAYS HE MADE YAHUAH THE SKIES AND THE ARETS

THE SEA AND ALL THAT IN THEM BUT HE RESTED ON THE DAY THE SEVENTH

FOR THIS HE BARUK YAHUAH DAY OF THE SHABATH AND HE MADE SEPARATE HIM

HONOR FATHER OF YOU AND MOTHER OF YOU THAT THEY MAY BE LONG DAYS OF YOU

IN THE LAND THAT YAHUAH ALAHIM OF YOU GIVING TO YOU

NOT YOU MURDER NOT YOU BREAK WEDLOCK NOT YOU STEAL

NOT YOU GIVE AGAINST NEIGHBOR OF YOU TESTIMONY DECEPTIVE

NOT YOU COVET HOUSE OF NEIGHBOR OF YOU NOT YOU COVET WIFE OF NEIGHBOR OF YOU

OR MANSERVANT OR MAIDSERVANT OR OX OR DONKEY OR ANYTHING OF YOUR NEIGHBOR

The Hebrew word for **neighbor** is RA, H7453:
RESH-AYIN. (Pronounced "RAY")
It means *companion, friend, associate*.
Watch a short video about this Hebrew word:
https://youtu.be/22aiOGhnNqM

IMAGE OF THE BEAST
CONSTANTINE'S SUN IDOL
THE CROSS

Constantine merged his Sun worship along with its
symbol, and it became the symbol of his universal
religion at Nicaea (325 CE). The dragon has
poisoned the minds of the inhabitants of Earth.
Sunday (dies solis) supplanted the day of rest under
the Edict of Constantine (313 CE), and all shops
were ordered closed under penalty of death. The
veneration (worship) of the Sun (Apollo, Rome's
name for Nimrod) became the day of rest during his
reign.
The world accepts this practice and many other
pagan habits because they are not warned.
At Yahusha's return, many unwise virgins will not
have enough oil to enter the marriage feast.

Concerning the last days and the great distress Yahusha mentioned at Mt. 24:20, what "Sabbath" was He speaking of, Constantine's transference of resting to his day of the Sun, or the real one on the seventh day of each week?

The plague of the last days will be very distressful. ZekarYah 14:12-21 says this:
"And this is the plague with which Yahuah plagues all the people who fought against Yerushalim: their flesh shall decay while they stand on their feet, and their eyes decay in their sockets, and their tongues decay in their mouths. And it shall be in that yom that a great confusion from Yahuah is among them, and everyone of them shall seize the hand of his neighbor, and his hand rise up against his neighbor's hand. And Yahudah shall fight at Yerushalim as well. And the wealth of all the guyim round about shall be gathered together: gold, and silver, and garments in great quantities. So also is the plague on the horse and the mule, on the camel and the donkey, and on all the cattle that are in those camps – as this plague. And it shall be that all who are left from all the Guyim which came up against Yerushalim, shall go up from year to year to bow themselves to the King, Yahuah Tsabauth, and to observe the Festival of Sukuth. And it shall be, that if anyone of the clans of the arets does not come up to Yerushalim to bow himself to the King, Yahuah Tsabauth, on them there is to be no rain. And if the clan of Mitsrim does not come up and enter in, then there is no rain. On them is the plague with which Yahuah plagues the

guyim who do not come up to observe the Festival of Sukuth. This is the punishment of Mitsrim and the punishment of all the guyim that do not come up to observe the Festival of Sukuth. In that yom "QODESH TO YAHUAH" shall be engraved on the bells of the horses. And the pots in the House of Yahuah shall be like the bowls before the altar. And every pot in Yerushalim and Yahudah shall be qodesh to Yahuah Tsabauth. And all those who slaughter shall come and take them and cook in them."

The use of the Hyksos / Hieroglyphs in the charts are being passed all around the Internet through teachers watching other teachers, and quite wrong. The use of foreign languages to define the meaning of Eberith words as they are transliterated into Latin letters is another huge misunderstanding. I've left a couple of comments in the video, and at first they were not received well, but hopefully eventually they will. The suffix SHUA is not my preferred transliteration, as SHA is used for both HUSHA and ALISHA. Here are my comments on that: Hieroglyphics is not a script used by the prophets in any of the Writings Of Truth, but has become very important to teachers on the Internet. As for the meaning of the suffix, shin-ayin (SHA), teachers differ in the contextual meaning of it, which is easily corrected when we study. It comes from the same root seen in the names Alisha (Elisha) and YashaYahu (Isaiah): YASHA (yod-shin-ayin). Shua means cry out, I agree, but when Mushah invented the word YAHUSHA, he only added a yod to what already existed, hay-uau-shin-ayin, HUSHA. There is not a SHUA in the name HUSHA, although after the Masoretes added their uninspired vowels to the word, it came to be JOSHUA in all the references following the KJV. Transliterating with babbling languages which were mutilated by foreign lips before we were born isn't easy to overcome. Yahuah became our Deliverer, Yahusha.

The suffix (SHA) uses the shin-ayin to mean "deliverer" from the root, YASHA.

(see also the name YashaYahu, aka "Isaiah").

The spelling yod-hay-uau-hay (Yahuah) is used in the TaNaK 6823 times in the Eberith Scriptures. Interlinear translations will verify the following:

Mushah (Moses) added the letter yod to his assistant's name: Y + HUSHA see Num. 13:16

Three spellings are found in the TaNaK for the same name given to our Mashiak:

1 time: yod-shin-uau-ayin (hypocorisma or diminutive form, YSHUA) see NekemYah 8:17

2 times: yod-hay-uau-shin-uau-ayin (YAHUSHUA) The two uses of this 6-lettered spelling are found at Deut. 3:21 and Judges. 2:7.

216 times: yod-hay-uau-shin-ayin (YAHUSHA) see ZekarYah 3

The predominant spelling is best to teach and use, since it is the one most likely devoid of scribal errors or directed attacks on Yahuah's Name written most often in the Scriptures of Truth. Close examination of the charts shown around the Internet combine real Eberith pictographic script with Hieroglyphic pictographs. The Hieroglyphic letters are not Eberith, and no physical evidence of them being used by Yisharal to write anything, and certainly not the Name, has ever been discovered.

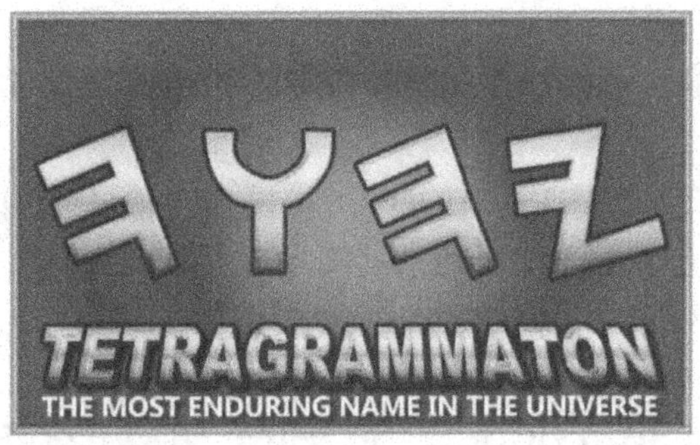

Tetragrammaton - The Most Enduring Name In The Universe
The ancient Hebrew script has been a secret.
A papal bull in 2008 forbade the sound of a Name based on 4 letters of that script.
That script has been suppressed and mislabeled with a Greek name, PHOENICIAN, a word invented by Herodotus, meaning "date palm." Herodotus was referring to the occupiers of the eastern Mediterranean Sea's coastal region occupied by a sea people that had many colonies. These folks were very advanced in their shipbuilding. Scholars today still call them Phoenicians; but they are the

tribes who eventually spread their writings across the Great Sea, and beyond. This book will show you their script, and reveal the Name hidden for ages, written in four letters, and called the Tetragrammaton.

Since Nimrod's original rebellion against Yahuah and the building of the Tower, our languages have become disheveled, confused, and obviously rendered unrecoverable because we turned away from our Creator's love.

Hebrew itself has been corrupted by marks invented in the 8th century CE, further diverting the pure language from being able to utter the Name of our Creator. This book focuses on the four lettered Name that scholars refer to as "four letters," or Tetragrammaton. It was written on a golden headpiece worn by the high priest, and only uttered aloud once each year in the most set-apart place in the world, next to the Ark of the Covenant.

Yusef Ben MatithYahu (aka Josephus) the first-century historian wrote that he saw the headpiece, and on it was written the the Name in "four vowels," and in the Eberith script (not Aramith). What were these letters, and why are they kept from the general population of Truth seekers?

This book displays those same "four vowels" on the cover. Malaki 3:16-18 reveals that those who meditate on this Name, and speak to one another, are a "treasured possession" and their names were written in a special "scroll of remembrance."

This book is only for a select few who meditate on that precious Name written in four vowels.

The enduring secrecy surrounding four Hebrew letters in their original form is without precedence among all other secrets on Earth.

In spite of this, the knowledge of Yahuah will be known as the waters cover the sea.

The Name is written so a generation yet to be created will call on the Name of Yahuah.

The Name is on display at the Shrine of the Book in Jerusalem, but few people recognize it. The central display holds the Great Isaiah Scroll, mostly written in Aramaic, and the Name Yahuah appears in Eberith, what is known today as Hebrew. Those four letters of the Name are described by scholars as the TETRAGRAMMATON - A Greek word meaning "four letters."

Few teachers know this, but the script most people call Hebrew (Eberith) is actually the script we brought back from our captors. The language (phonology) is Eberith, but the Aramith script is used to transliterate the sound of the words. We transliterate Hebrew words using Latin letters all the time (example: SHALOM). Because Aramith is a transliteration, the Masoretes added phonemes (niqqud marks) in the 8th century CE to guide the reader. There are no such marks in any of the Dead Sea Scrolls, and many words have been radically altered after the 8th century; none more so than the Name of Yahuah, the four vowels known as the Tetragrammaton. Yahuah's Name should have no gnats or skidmarks around it.

MASORETIC VOWELS

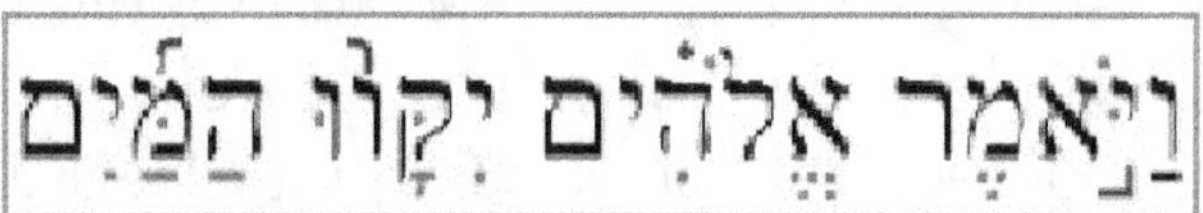

ARAMAIC LETTERS WITH NIQQUD MARKS
THIS IS NOT HEBREW
TORAH INSTITUTE

What Is The Name Of Deliverance?

Acts 4:12 informs us of a very important Name. The only Name given among men by which we must be delivered finds its source in the Eberith language, and when *written* in Eberith script, anyone may use the source to learn how to pronounce it (Psalm 102:18).

The Name YAHUSHA is based on the four vowels yod-hay-uau-hay (YAHUAH), with a suffix added using two letters, shin-ayin. The four letters yod-hay-uau-hay are vowels, and only involve the mouth cavity and breath. The suffix (shin-ayin) is a modifier, adding "deliverer" to the Name. This suffix can be seen in the name ALISHA as well. Teaching the Name involves studying the Eberith script and using the letters to make intelligible words. Most people asking to learn "Hebrew" are shown the Aramaic script, and the phonemes indicating additional vowel sounds (niqqud marks) introduced in the 8th century by a sect of Karaites by the name Masoretes.

A crescent-Moon confirms a fully-built first day of a month, but it is commonly mistaken to be the beginning point of a month. The sighted-crescent Moon was adopted from the Islamic process by Anan, the founder of the Karaite sect in Babel (767 CE). The Hebrew word for Moon is YERAK, and is often confused with the word KODESH, which is the period of a month as we know it. The word for FULL (KESEH, H3677 at Psalm 81:3) Moon is used 1 time in a phase describing a confirmed sighting of the object itself, on the day of our festival. The teachers need to study more so there will be less confusion about this, and many other points as well.

Those teaching the FULLY illuminated Moon is the renewal point for a month overlook not only the pattern of every culture on Earth, but also the mention of the "day of our festival" at Psalm 81:3. Sukkoth is not observed in total darkness, but displays the appearance of a Great Light. It is contrasted with the day of the shout when the 7th KODESH (month) is renewed; the shofar is blown on both the 1st and the 15th within the same period, exactly 15 days apart. The fully illuminated disk is on the 15th. Counting back to the 1st, it becomes obvious there was no Moon to see at all.

1 Shemual 20:18 shows how they knew ***"tomorrow is the KODESH"*** (a new month, H2320).

Gardening helps us learn about Yahuah's Creation. To receive seed, the soil must be ready, and planted at the proper time.

Phyllis and I have only been learning to garden for the last 4 years. There are many advantages to growing in buckets and containers, often layered within one another. Water retention, composting-in-place, and keeping the drain holes 2" from the bottom keeps out tree roots seeking the nutrients and/or blocking-up the drain holes. Tree roots reach out 30-50 or more feet in search of water, and yet we like our forest next to our garden. We use wood chips everywhere, and as they break down, they enrich the whole environment. We use tree leaves all year to cover the soil surface in the containers, and they provide protection and nutrients as they slowly release the minerals they contain from their tree's roots which were carried up from deep underground. It's a self-sustaining "no-dig" method of gardening that we love to watch. A few well-place bird baths and feeders attract enough birds to eat any garden pests that may pose a threat, and a few little ponds provide dragon flies and frogs to finish-off even more pests. Yahuah has created so many magnificent and wonderful things.

Yahusha is our Passover, the Lamb of Alahim. He is the Redeemer from beginning to end in the Scriptures of Truth. His indwelling destroys the works of the devil, not His Commandments. *Those who know Him guard and teach them.* The remembrance of His death on the 14th between the evenings (nearing sunset prior to the 15th) is observed by all immersed followers of His teachings. The beginning of the 14th of the first month also holds great meaning to His last Natsarim alive today. Nearing sunset on the 13th, we observe the example of the remembrance supper He had with His followers as we read His final instructions to the first Natsarim before His death. From the beginning to the end of the 14th, we meditate on the time He took the bread and the cup of wine, prayed in the garden, was arrested and mistreated all night and the following day. After Yahusha finished His last meal with His first Natsarim, He had already begun to die. As He prayed fervently in the garden, He was shedding blood in His sweat. Every drop that He spilled counts, and every moment leading up to His final breath the next afternoon is part of the remembrance each of us cherish dearly. Yahusha's last Natsarim are here on the Earth again, appealing to all mankind: be restored to favor.

Where is the Ark?
Revelation 11 tells us the Ark of the Covenant is safely resting in Yahusha's possession. It hasn't been seen on the earth since the first Temple was destroyed. If it were in Phoenix, Arizona - Nairobi, Kenya - Rockwall, Texas - or anywhere where a man could walk up and touch it, that man would not survive that touch. What is inside the Ark (box) is even more qodesh: the Ketubah itself (stone tablets written by the finger of Yahuah). The blood of Yahusha is the offering to end all animal blood offerings, and His blood is now sprinkled on the hearts of those who believe and obey the Covenant. The Lamb is coming back to reign with His bride, and His Natsarim are announcing to the world to prepare for Him. An invitation to the marriage supper of the Lamb is offered; who will believe our report? Repent; for the reign of Yahuah draws near! Baruk haba baShem Yahuah!

Christianese Has Distorted The Besorah
Consider what you have not heard.

Those who obey receive the Spirit of Yahusha (Acts 5:32), and He helps us to understand, and do the things that are pleasing to Him by the power of His Spirit living in us.

Demons believe, but they do not obey. Repenting means to turn from sin, and trust in the perfect offering of Yahusha's blood that cleanses us from our past sins, and the penalty of death required for those sins.

We pledge ourselves to Him by the act of immersion, calling on the one Name (Yahusha, Acts 4:12) for the forgiveness of our crimes against His eternal Covenant. If we claim we know Him, and do not guard His Commandments, we lie, and the Truth (His Word) is not in us (1 Yn. 3:4). The "old" covenant was written a scroll and placed beside the ark, and that old priesthood and the prescribed animal blood is no longer functional (See Dt. 31:26, Hebrews 6:13). Animal blood is imperfect to redeem anyone.

The renewed Covenant is cut, and our minds are circumcised by our belief in Yahusha's blood which He has given for us.

He has redeemed us completely by His own blood, the one perfect offering as our High Priest. The Ruach ha Qodesh gave Himself to purchase us with His own blood (Acts 20:28).

Who Were You Taught To Call On For Deliverance?

3000 People Were Immersed After Hearing These Words (Acts 2:38):

"Repent and be immersed, every one of you, in the Name of Yahusha Mashiak for the forgiveness of yours sins, and you will receive the gift of the Ruach ha Qodesh."

You only need Yahusha and a pool of water to be immersed, He is the One you have to call on for **deliverance**, and then you will see others as He sees them. Where His Ruach dwells, love dwells.

If you love Yahusha, obey Him, and keep your eyes fixed on Him, or you'll sink. May the workers in His harvest increase the moment you come up from the waters!

Zodiac Madness

The constellations / zoo imagined to be in the *host of heaven* worshiped by the nations are what Yahuah refers to in the 2nd Commandment, and evokes a very high degree of jealous rage in Him to see His children misled by them, or to pay any attention to them. They are not real, only imagined. The worship of the *host of heaven* is the old astrology system from Babel, and Stephen warned the assembly about it at Acts 7:42. YirmeYahu (Jer.)

10:2 and Ayub (Job) 31:27 show us Yahuah's perspective on the subject. Even the elect may be enticed into thinking these practices from Babel are indicators of Yahusha's return. Flee from these concepts, and warn others: anathema! maranathah! (forbidden! Master comes!)
http://fossilizedcustoms.com/zodiac.html

Do Not Learn The Ways Of The Heathen
As we perform a careful study of the festivals of Yahuah, Enoch is not mentioned in them. They represent the outline (shadow) of Yahuah's redemption plan for all who seek and obey Him. The confusion among teachers on the calendar is an ever-expanding alternate universe where crowds are following cross-pollinated teachings based on Kabbalah, Jewish mysticism, and a rich blend of Babel's zoo animals.
Images in the skies, or a *heavenly scroll*, are believed to contain messages about mankind's redemption plan, and Yahusha's return to reign. These things are forbidden by the second Commandment. YirmeYahu 10 explicitly tells us not to learn the things the nations fear. The worship of the *host of heaven* was mentioned by Stephen before they took him out and stoned him to death for uttering the Name of Yahuah. (Acts 7)
The word *imagination* is based on the word image. Teachers *imagine*, and those who listen to them are *confused*. Look at YashaYahu 44:25, and surrounding verses. The practice of counting the omer is not found in Scripture, but calculating the 7 weeks between First-Fruits and Shabuoth is easy to understand by reading Uyiqara 23 & Debarim 16. Yahuah's appointed times are easy when read from

His Word, not explained by teachers. They are
Yahuah's redemption plan for all mankind.
From First-Fruits during Matsah to the 50th day
after is the calculation for Shabuoth. The unfulfilled
appointed times occur in the 7th month, ushering-in
the reign of Yahusha. The annual observances, or
appointed times, are described on this card:

The Passover in Mitsrayim foreshadowed the
slaughtering of the Lamb of Alahim. There is no
Redeemer besides Yahuah, and He purchased us
by offering Himself as the atonement for the sins of
the whole world (Acts 20:28). He did not end or
overcome His Commandments, but He overcame
the works of the devil. All the appointed times during
the year, beginning with PESAK, are the redemption
plan. These are the "shadows of things to come." In
the coming reign of Yahusha, and even now, one

can distinguish between those who serve Alahim and those who do not serve Him. (See Malaki 3:17-18 & context)

Are The Sabbath & Week Lost?

No, they are not lost, but they are constantly under attack. The week, the month, and the year are being revised and re-interpreted by a growing number of believers in Yahusha. The fragmenting is on-going, and heartbreaking to watch.

The Roman calendar uses a completely incorrect way of identifying time, and think to alter the beginning of their days, their years, and their months (Dan. 7:25). Rome tried to alter the weeks also, but the seven pillars of time set forth from the beginning of Creation could not be altered even by the 4th beast (Proverbs 9:1). They tried an 8-day week, but it evaporated. All other imaginary designs will fail as well. If the Covenant sign (Shabath) ever fades from mankind's memory, a six-day manna-feeding program might appear as it did for Yisharal during the 40 years in the desert. It's far too important for us to expect Yahuah to use a cartoon drawing to reset the week, yet we see cartoon teaching props being used all over the Internet.

The 7th day and the week have never been lost to those who have lived over the generations with the Covenant sign of Shabath. Yahusha referred to the Shabath day still being observed just before He returns when He said, "pray your flight not be . . . on the Shabath." (Mt. 24:20)

Is "Count" A Verb Or Noun?

Someone recently asked about the "counting of the omer" tradition, and wondered about the traditional word Pentecost. The Hebrew is the true source, but the Greek and Latin influences cause distortions. *Pentecost* means *"count fifty"* in Greek, and is an invented word through translation referring to **Shabuoth** (weeks). The Greek word Pentecost is a compound word having two components. *Peninta* is the Greek word for fifty. *Komitos* is the medieval Greek for "count," from KOMIS. The Latinized form of *Komitos* produces the cost component we've inherited. The Hebrew Roots of our belief, and most words, steer us away from the path of truth, but with careful study we can restore a better understanding.

The Hebrew Word "Count"

SEPARTIM (H5608) is a verb meaning count, number, enumerate, calculate, or reckon, and it's used in verses 15 & 16 of Uyiqara (Lev.) 23. In verse 15 we calculate SHEBA SHABATHUTH (7 Sabbaths) from the Wave Sheaf offering; in verse 16 the word is used again in reference to the sum of fifty days by including the day following the 7th Shabath. This makes it certain that the date of Shabuoth is always on a first day of a week, and reflects the pattern of the Shemitah (7th year rest for the land) and the fiftieth year when property ownership is restored in the year of Yobel (Jubilee).

To the Torah and to the Witness!

Riots in many cities after dark are going on recently. Marauding bands of violent inciters travel to these places to bring chaos among otherwise peaceful protesters. The spiritual side of these events is obviously the true source of the evil being unleashed. Summer heat, the economic collapse from coronavirus-induced job losses, and the media constantly reporting on unlawful actions by a small number of the law enforcement community provide conditions for a perfect storm, even in otherwise peaceful cities where nothing is wrong. Evil spirits are real, and enter into anyone's house (mind) not inhabited by the Spirit of Yahusha. The lawless is increasing because the pastors teach a bitterness toward obedience, making the way of Truth seem to be evil (2 Peter 2:2). School teachers are not allowed to teach the Ten Commandments of kindness to the children. The end of days is at hand, therefore be watchful and take every opportunity to teach the Name of Yahuah and His Word to all you possibly can. Read about the solution from Malachi 4:1-6, and ask pastors why they have failed to teach this solution.

False Worship Abounds
Indoor altars, images, monstrances, bowing, lighting candles like Hindus with prayers associated with them, sacraments, Bel towers, cruxes, wreaths, tree decorating, hand gestures, prayers to dead (necromancy), bead-praying, holy water, zodiacs, and so many other false teachings will be the fuel for the fire coming on the Earth. Yahusha is the only - the one Name - we must call on for the forgiveness of our crimes against Him, and He is the Creator and Possessor of Shamayim and Arets. The builders rejected the Stone, His Name, and every false translation proves this.
Read the Preface of your translation. His Name is not LORD or any other device; He says, "I am Yahuah; that is My Name!" (YashaYahu 42:8)

Is Jesus The Antichrist? (Another Yahusha)
https://youtu.be/CKC47PQXV_4
 (youtube video with this author)

The Truth sounds ridiculous at first, yet it will be shown to be self-evident after careful study.

There is only one Name given under heaven among men by which we must be delivered (Acts 4:12). Men invented the name JESUS, but the true Mashiak came to destroy the works of the devil, not Yahuah's Commandments. The whole world is deceived. Yahusha is the one Name by which we are Delivered, and it means *"I am your Deliverer."* What does Jesus mean?
Natsarim guard the Name and the Word.
Yeh-Zus is the Antichrist, the lawless one coming in an impostor's name.

The pastors of Christianity don't understand what the renewed Covenant is. When they explain what they think it is, we are told to stay away from the Ten Commandments, or else we are will think we are earning our deliverance! Yahusha helps us see what is good, and as the Paraklita (Helper) gives us the strength to obey them, and we see how the "way of Truth" has been maligned (2 Peter 2:2). The "old" Covenant was not about redemption, but rather animal blood temporarily covered crimes through the old priesthood offering it year by year for the unintentional crimes. This *old covenant* was written on a scroll (Dt. 31:26), and place *beside* the ark.
The text explaining the *change* of this law of sin and death, and the change in the priesthood, is explained at Hebrews 8:13. Yahusha's blood redeemed all who turn back to obedience, accepting His perfect offering of Himself. Our list of crimes is wiped clean: Cheirographon - *What is it?*

This study will equip you with information you never realized you needed. Download the tract by this title at **www.torahzone.net** – it's free.

You will discover secrets that seminary-trained teachers never told you because they use mind-scrubbing therapies on crowds, not raw Truth.
In the BYNV, Danial 8:12-13 reads:
"And because of transgression, an army was given over to the horn to oppose that which is continual. And it threw the Truth down to the ground, and it acted and prospered. Then I heard a certain qodesh one speaking. And another qodesh one said to that certain one who was speaking, "Till when is the vision, concerning that which is continual, and the transgression that lays waste, to make both the qodesh place and the host to be trampled under foot?"

Gabrial describes the *duration of desolation*, and the *time of the end*. The word TAMID (H8548) is found in verses 11 and 13. As I've translated it in the BYNV, the word **continual** is a better understanding for us than *sacrifices* or *daily*.
The same word can mean different things depending on what it is referring to.
The *regular operation* of the qodesh place is being referred to, and now it is being trampled (desolated) underfoot by the invaders. Continual control over the place where Yahuah placed His Name was lost, and now the image of the **destroyer** (the dome, or shivalingam) has been built in the place where it should not be.

More about the Abomination of Desolation, which is already "set up" (built):
fossilizedcustoms.com/abomination.html

I Was Educated By The Jesuit-Illuminati

Yes; I was educated by Loyola's Societas IESV from a young age, yet I perceived something behind it all that caused me to doubt the veracity of the authority the "order" claimed to have. The order goes by many names, and there is a video I recommend you watch to expose more of their aims to control the world. They are highly-skilled infiltrators, but I assure you I was never a follower of their programming. Here's a link to a video about the World Order from the perspective of one who was educated by the Jesuit-Illuminati:
https://youtu.be/20QZB4-f0lc

Test What You Are Taught

Often, it is by questioning teachings we come to a knowledge of the Truth. *When was the last time you heard a pastor give a sermon on 1 Yn. 2:3-7?*

"And by this we know that we know Him, if we guard His commands. The one who says, "I know Him," and does not guard His commands, is a liar, and the truth is not in him. But whoever guards His Word, truly the love of Yahuah has been perfected in him. By this we know that we are in Him. The one who says he lives in Him ought himself also to walk even as He walked. Beloved, I write no original unfamiliar command to you, but an old command which you have had from the beginning. The old command is the Word which you heard from the beginning."

Can a person obey the Ten Commandments and still use foreign names for Yahuah?
Most likely if a person began to live by them his assembly would ask him not to come back among them. Christians are taught not to obey them, yet Yahusha lived by them and taught them. He is also the Helper Who guides us in them. Assemblies are taught to guard the traditions of their pastors. Yahusha's followers were given their name by Yahusha Himself:

"I am the Vine; you are the Natsarim."
ANI HA GAFEN; ATAH HA NATSARIM

Paul was accused of being a ringleader of the Natsarim at Acts 24:5. He also claimed that he followed the Torah, and in fact agreed with the Torah as a way of life, not his former life, the traditions of the fathers. He no longer walked as an anti-missionary, a Natsarim-slayer. The translators removed the Name of Yahuah from the texts, and they admit doing so in their Prefaces. The word JESUS did not exist until the 17th century, and is a replacement name the world has accepted. Questions serve a good purpose, and I hope everyone keeps asking them.

Whom Do You Seek?

The hearts of Yahusha's followers are the ARK containing the Ten Words He made us love. His Name seals us at our immersion as His property. For those looking for His Temple, look no further; we are His Dwelling Place. Yahusha said, "I am the Vine; you are the Natsarim."
Unless Yahuah builds the house, the builders labor in vain (Ps. 127:1). Yahusha's Name seals us for the day of the redemption of our bodies, His living stones. The *Spirit* and the *bride* says, *"come."*

Space weather is driven by what's going on with the Sun, and one super flare is 10,000 times more burning energy than a normal solar flare. The solar winds are pouring-out of holes opening up on the Sun's surface. Sudden destruction is inevitable, explaining why the governments are building D.U.M.B.'s - tunnels you can research.

Last Natsarim Reunited - New effort on youtube - subscribe quick, hit the bell, and share it.
https://youtu.be/v06CaMSZs6Y

The days will be shorten for the sake of the elect, but we are about to see it all around us.

More Resources

Margaret St. Peter talks about how she was inspired to write her first book in a video interview with Phyllis and Lew White.

She was searching diligently for the Truth, and did not give up. What she found was so compelling and real, she had to tell everyone that she could, and started to plan a website. It turned into the book:

4 Steps Through The Narrow Gate - This Is The Way, Walk In It.

Margaret hopes this book will help people find the Truth. https://youtu.be/2BgGOXLrGC0

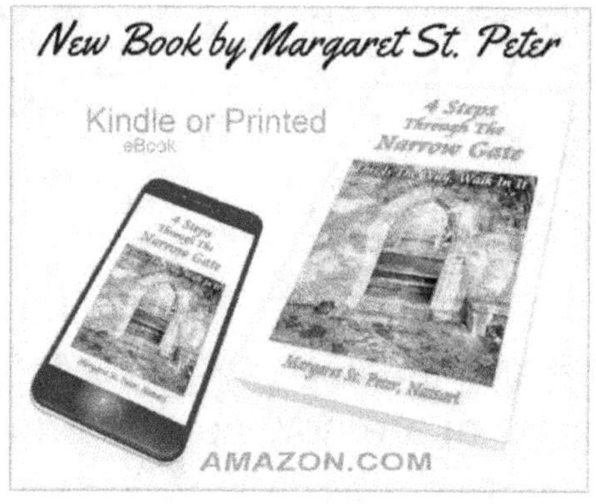

You can download these eBooks in seconds.

Love is a book containing the Introduction and Glossary found in the BYNV translation.

Last Natsarim are now here to bring the

final warning to all inhabitants of the Earth.
The reign of Yahusha is near.

NO CANDY HERE SIGN PDF 24" x 24"
Show the lost what Halloween looks like from
Yahusha's perspective.
Use the PDF for making posters, yard-signs, sharing
in email blasts, and whatever you like. Christmas,
Easter, Halloween, Valentine's Day, birthday cakes,
Sun-day, and other practices are highly thought of
among men, but abominations in the sight of Yahuah
(Luke 16:14-15). People learned these as children,
and most never break the spell of their stronghold.

AMBASSAFLASH – 16GB FLASHDRIVE
USB Mass Storage Device
Over 100 tracts as PDF, plus over 20 MP4 instructional videos
ORDER FROM TORAHZONE.NET

Instructions for printing tracts:

Tracts are formatted for landscape, double-sided, do not shrink, black ink on white paper.

For cards and signs, follow uploading instructions (we recommend Vistaprint).

Each tract has 4 pages, and a few front pages are shown below; if this is the eBook, expand each photo.
Download selected tracts FREE: torahzone.net.
After registering, add titles to your cart, and an email will be sent to you with a link for you to download your selections.

FALL OF BABEL

AT THE TIME OF THE END

The world has been led to expect a far different outcome than will actually be experienced. The Scripture of Truth describes a very rebellious and disobedient population in the last days, and those thinking they will be justified for believing, and not *obeying*, will be in for the shock of their lives. ***Get ready for the ride of your life.***

A little flock of Yahusha's ambassadors are leading many to His **Name**, to *obey* His **Commandments**, calling them to turn from **idolatry**, and be delivered. This is the order given by Him to the first Natsarim (Mt. 28:20), and now He is awakening the last Natsarim through the pressures (distress) in these last days. Like the plagues He sent on the disobedient Egyptians, the whole world will watch the fulfillment of 2 Kronicles 7:13-15, Dan. 12, YashaYahu / Is. 24, and Mt. 24:11-13.

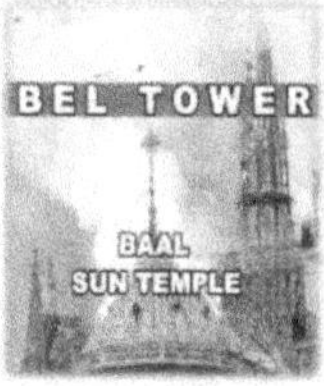

Get out of the circus, reapers are coming!

A Covenant With Death

Pastors have removed The Name from their translations, and trained their assemblies to be disobedient and lawless, validation that they have made a ***covenant with death***. All of them are blind to the idolatry, and ignore Yahuah's instructions. ***"Therefore hear the Word of Yahuah, you men of scorn, who rule this people who are in Yerushalim, because you have said, 'We have made a covenant with death, and with the grave we have effected a vision. When the overflowing scourge passes through, it does not come to us, for we have made lying our refuge, and under falsehood we have hidden ourselves.' Therefore thus said Aduni Yahuah, 'See, I am laying in Tsiun a Stone for a foundation, a tried Stone, a precious corner-stone, a settled foundation. He who trusts shall not hasten away. And I shall make lawfulness the measuring line, and obedience the plummet. And the hail shall sweep away the refuge of lies, and the mayim overflow the hiding place. And your covenant with death shall be annulled, and your vision with the grave not stand.***

PAGE 1 OF 4 GET TRACT FREE AT TORAHZONE.NET

THE REAL NAME

TRANSLITERATIONS

	6,823	216	2	1
	YAHUAH	**YAHUSHA**	**YAHUSHUA**	**Y'SHUA**
HEBREW	[illegible]	[illegible]	[illegible]	[illegible]
ARAMAIC	יהוה	יהושע	יהושוע	ישוע
GREEK	IAOUE	IHSOUS		
LATIN	IEHOUAH	IESU		

AT HEBREWS 4 AND ACTS 7 THE SAME GREEK LETTERING IS USED FOR "JOSHUA" AND "JESUS" - IHSOUS
THIS IS CONFIRMATION BOTH WERE CALLED YAHUSHA IN HEBREW
TORAH INSTITUTE

ONE OF THESE TWO IS OF RECENT ORIGIN, AND THEREFORE A FRAUD:

JESUS OR YAHUSHA?

"YAHUSHA" means "Yah is our deliverer" in Hebrew. "JESUS" seems to convey *"hail Zeus"* in Greek, and ***"the horse"*** in Hebrew *(HE-SOOS)*.

Both cannot be true. Since there was no letter "J" on planet Earth until around 1530 CE, one of these two is already exposed as a hoax.
To say ***"we speak English"*** isn't a defense of anything, since the "only **Name**" given by which there is deliverance is a Hebrew Name, not an English one (Acts 4:12).
The Latin letters we use for the correct sound of the Name to call upon are called "English", but "Jesus" isn't an English word. Jesus is a Latinized form of Greek, taken from IESOUS into the Latin Vulgate as IESU. Yahuah does not change, so the Name of our Mashiak would not undergo alterations over time, so it was tampered with by an enemy. The Anti-messiah will come in the name Jesus.

Scholars know how to determine the real Name of the Mashiak of Israel, but they hesitate because *tradition* would be challenged. The evidence reveals that the person known as "Joshua" in the Scriptures has exactly the same Hebrew name as the Mashiak, because both the Mashiak and the successor of Mosheh are identical in Greek, **IESOUS**. The Name of the Mashiak is not Greek, but Hebrew.
The Name has a meaning in Hebrew; yet "JESUS" (or JEZUS if in Jugoslavia) is promoted by the **Society of Jesus** (Jesuits) to be valid based solely upon Greek, not Hebrew. This study should set the record straight, because we are going to look at the Hebrew to allow the true Name to become known.
The intermediate languages have only mutilated the original for us.

YAHUSHA & YAHUSHUA ARE BOTH CORRECT TRANSLITERATIONS

THE MASHIAK'S NAME IS FOUND **219 TIMES** IN THE TANAK.
In 216 of these, the spelling is: **yod-hay-uau-shin-ayin: YAHUSHA.**
The *son of Nun* (a leader of the tribe Ephraim / Afraim) that we find in the concordance started out with a four-lettered name, then Mosheh changed it by adding *one letter* (YOD) to the *beginning* of his name:

#1954: HAY-UAU-SHIN-AYIN (HUSHA), rendered in the KJV as HOSHEA (Dt. 32:44), and OSHEA (Num 13:16).

PAGE 1 OF 4

TURNED ASIDE TO MYTHS

WHAT ARE THEY, WHO'S DOING IT, AND WHAT COULD POSSIBLY GO WRONG?

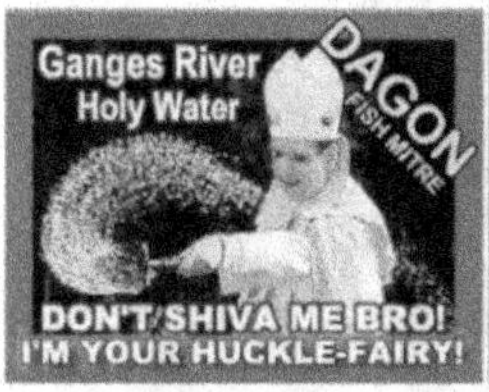

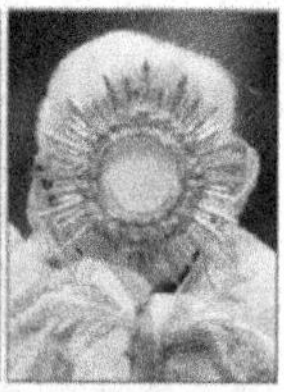

WHY DOES CHRISTIANITY LOOK LIKE SUN WORSHIP?

Sound doctrines are all now replaced by traditions of men. Futility, lies, and myths have filled the earth with customs people embrace as familiar, and the Truth has become thought of as evil. Paul wrote of these things to Timothy: **"Proclaim the Word! Be urgent in season, out of season. Correct, warn, appeal, with all patience and teaching.**
For there shall be a time when they shall not bear sound teaching, but according to their own desires, they shall heap up for themselves teachers tickling the ear, and they shall indeed turn their ears away from the Truth, and be turned aside to myths." 2Timothy 4:2-4
A myth is a widely-held belief, among these are sacraments, holy water, transubstantiation, Sun-day, Trinities, celibacy, image worship, popes, nuns, monks, steeples, obelisks, wreaths, lent, chants, special days, prayers to the dead, indulgences, pilgrimages, stigmatas, Easter egg hunts, Dec. 25th Solstice birth, Santa, elves, trees in homes, monstrances, bells, and all forms of fertility patterns of Babel.

TEACHING AS TEACHINGS THE COMMANDS OF MEN

Luke reports for us in Acts about many events spanning about 32 years after the death and resurrection of Yahusha. He describes many of the challenges faced by his fellow traveler and convert we know as Paul. Paul was *formerly* known as Shaul, who had been given authority by the Sanhedrin to arrest the Natsarim (branches) in the assemblies found to be uttering Yahuah's Name, which they called blasphemy. Shaul was confronted by Yahusha in Person on his way to Damascus. Paul was gifted with skills and mentored by Gamliel. Gamaliel was the grandson of the noble Torah teacher Hillel. Paul was able to speak to anyone who would listen, and was not intimidated in the least by any lawyers, judges, sophists, governors or kings.

PAGE 1 OF 4 - GET ENTIRE TRACT: TORAHZONE.NET

TETRAGRAMMATON

THIS IS MY NAME FOREVER

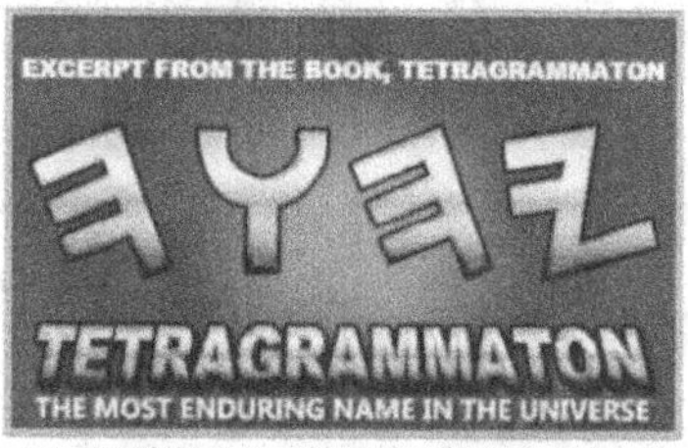

Transliterating The Four Vowels

A Name Hidden For Ages

Transliteration uses letters to make a word sound the same using foreign scripts. **Vowels** are sounded using only the mouth cavity and breath. What is a vowel, and how do they differ from consonants?
A vowel is a letter sounded without the lips, lower lip with upper teeth, closed teeth, hissing, tongue on the roof of the mouth, or guttural stop in the throat. The shape of the mouth cavity is used. If we hear buzzing, hissing, clicking, or the tongue stops the air as in the word *giggle*, you are making the sound of a consonant.
The Name of our Creator is written in four vowels: yod-hay-uau-hay, sounded as YAHUAH, not *YEHOVAH*. *"VEE"* is not a letter in the Tetragrammaton. The Latin letter V sounded as our U. VENUS (a false deity) was pronounced *UENUS*. The Greek letters **IAOUE**

Some sample content of tracts you can download free (first pages shown here).
Or get them all quickly; there are over 100 tracts on the AMBASSADISC digital library.
Each tract is 4 pages, and formatted to print double-sided on a single sheet of paper.

IDOLATRY

MANKIND'S MOST PROMINENT ACTIVITY

MANKIND'S DEFINITION
Extreme admiration, love, or revering of something or someone; worship of a physical object or person.

YAHUAH'S DEFINITION
Setting one's thoughts or actions on anything above Yahuah. He gives an example for us from His prophets, such as YashaYahu (Isaiah) 44:16.

IDOL EXAMPLES: politicians / rulers; movie or music idols; statues, pillars, toasting with drinks; prayers to any entities other than Yahuah, spirits, dead people (necromancy, beads). Expressions we hear used all the time in conversations, and the things we run out to buy and decorate with show how invested we are in all the witchcraft, and hardly ever associate them with idolatry: rosaries, steeples horseshoes and rabbits' feet for good luck - bringing trees into our homes to celebrate a birthday, Black F-day, "let's keep our fingers crossed," horoscopes, palmistry, fortune cookies, baking cakes for birthdays, cone hats, toasting, blowing-out candles, wishes, eggs in baskets and rabbits in the spring, sunrise services, giving candy to costumed children on the day of the dead, Valentine's Day gifts, cards, hearts, and using decorations that remind everyone that we encourage the idolatry that drives the world's economy. The golden cup of Babel has caused madness!

DRIVING THE WORLD ECONOMY

Every merchant prospers from the fertility celebrations that hardly anyone perceives because they are all hypnotized from a lifetime of exposure to the traditions handed-down from our fathers to children. Idolatry is exactly what Yahusha referred to as **stumbling blocks** at Mt. 18:3-8. Idolatry is taught to <u>children</u>, and passes into each new generation through family bonding.

Yahuah is sending the plagues now, but most people remain clueless to why.
Revelation 9:20
"And the rest of mankind, who were not killed by these plagues, did not repent of the works of their hands, that they should not worship the demons, and idols of gold, and of silver, and of brass, and of stone, and of wood, which are neither able to see, nor to hear, nor to walk. Merchants exploit the wormwood that causes the masses to stay drunk on the idolatrous fertility traditions.

LAST NATSARIM

AMBASSADORS OF THE REIGN OF YAHUSHA

NATSARIM ARE VERY REAL

We were prophesied to appear by YirmeYahu 31:6, and Revelation 12:17 explains as are the first-fruits, enraging the dragon because we obey the Commandments of Alahim and hold the Testimony of Yahusha. Christianity was born at Alexandria, Egypt, and reinforced by the authority of Rome beginning at Nicaea in 325 CE. The Natsarim were based at Antioch just prior to the destruction of the Temple, and had to hide themselves from the Magisterium for over 1300 years. We were forced to dwell in the hills and valleys, and called Passagians, Albigensians, Waldenses, and Huguenots. We are proclaiming the Name of Yahusha around the world as His envoys. A Catholic website mentioned this author's name, and I attempted to answer their questions about the Natsarim, but was blocked permanently. I saved the discourse we had up to that point, and now share it with you.

Has Anyone Heard Of The Cult Of The Natsarim?

CATHOLIC FORUM TOPIC: NATSARIM
Because my name, Lew White, came up on a Catholic forum, I registered to respond to several questions being asked about what they referred to as "the cult of the Natsarim." This is the entire, but brief, interaction I had with the Jesuits. You will find their final response very interesting.

Jesuit question to the forum:
Has anyone heard of the cult of the Natsarim? What are its core beliefs and how does it relate to Jewish and Christian religion??

My reply: The term Natsarim is used to describe the original followers of Yahusha of Natsarith at Acts 24:5.

CHRISTIANS ARE IN TROUBLE

PASTORS ARE LEARNING ABOUT THEIR TRADITIONS

"Christians Are In Trouble" - says a resigned pastor . . .

Christian pastors are beginning to learn there is something very wrong with their traditions. They perceive a circular pattern in their festivals, then discover the outward crust is only masking the pagan origins of their practices: the worship of the host of heaven. Christmas, New Year, Valentines, Easter, Mother & Father Days, and Halloween are celebrated world-wide, and all the merchants promote each of these **fertility festivals** many weeks ahead to exploit the sleeping hypnotized crowds. Their pastors sit and watch, never blowing the shofar to warn anyone. Their doctrines are built on sand, not based on the Scripture of Truth, so their witness is without a firm foundation. **If you begin to do what is written in the Word, they ask you NOT TO ATTEND their assembly.**
Christian pastors are resigning all around the world in order to serve Yahusha, not their denomination's orders. They are renouncing their 'ordination' to teach lies.
One pastor actually stated that

READ THE GLOBAL CURSE AT MAL. 4
CANCEL YOUR COVENANT WITH DEATH
BE RESTORED TO FAVOR

Christians are in trouble:
"We want to come into more understanding about certain doctrines and desire to be baptized in the Name of our Savior Yahusha to the [esteem] of Yahuah. Myself in Christianity was a preacher with general license. My wife and I resigned from this religion on 12-11-18. On 14 December we came shockingly into the understanding that Christianity is false and **Christians are in trouble."**
Danial 12, Mt. 24, and Malaki 4 are being recognized by those hearing the call of Yahusha. Those who know Him abide in His Word, and they know the Truth. All else is witchcraft (rebellion).

BEWARE THE BLOB

DESCRIBING THE LAST DAYS · YIRMEYAHU 16:19

ITS PURPOSE IS TO MAKE MORE OF ITSELF

"Beware the leaven of the Pharisees"

The 1958 movie, The Blob, could be a metaphor for how religion takes on a life of its own, and everyone is absorbed into it. The purpose of its existence is to make more of itself.
YirmeYahu 16:19 shows we've inherited lies through traditions handed-down to us. Religion is tradition, and it develops over time as it corrupts itself by men guided by their minds of flesh. Yahusha's yoke is light, without ritual, liturgy, or hierarchy. We have direct access to His love. He created each of us to be His companions, and His Torah is instruction for us how to love Him, and how to love our neighbor. Torah points to the ideal relationship for bearing the perfect fruit of good behavior.
Religious tradition is like the Blob blindly performing its purpose of absorbing, growing, and competing for dominance.
The **Covenant** is the marriage we will celebrate at the marriage supper, and *the Blob serves the purpose of annihilating it.* Our choice is between the **Covenant** (life), or the **Blob** (death).

RABBINICAL JUDAISM
Question: What is the leaven, or yeast of the Pharisees?
Answer: Rabbinic Judaism, the *traditions of the fathers.*

Some sample content of tracts you can download free (first pages shown here).
Or get them all quickly; there are over 100 tracts on the AMBASSADISC digital library.
Each tract is 4 pages, and formatted to print double-sided on a single sheet of paper.

AWAKENING THE WATCHMEN

"For the people shall dwell in Tsiun at Yerushalim, you shall weep no more. He shall show much favor to you at the sound of your cry; when He hears, He shall answer you. Though Yahuah gave you bread of adversity and water of affliction, your Teacher shall no longer be hidden. But your eyes shall see your Teacher, and your ears hear a word behind you, saying, "This is the Way, walk in it," whenever you turn to the right, or whenever you turn to the left. And you shall defile the covering of your graven images of silver, and the plating of your moulded images of gold. You shall throw them away as a menstrual cloth and say to them, "Be gone!" - YashaYahu 30:19-22 BYNV

This calling-out from the pigsty is happening as Yahusha's Ruach ha Qodesh pours into men and women. He is calling them away from the circuses, bells, steeples, candles, Sun-day meetings, and all the rest of the traditions of men. Challenge yourself to listen.

A PERSONAL TESTIMONY

This is how Yahusha turned me around: reading His Word of Truth. Pastors insist we read it, but never to obey what it says. They know the Truth is powerful; but like wizards, they want to be the *controllers of that power.* They were so repulsed when they heard me tell them I love obeying and teaching others to obey, they went to work destroying my reputation, warning others to avoid me. In the late 1990's, a conference of Texan pastors was called to discuss what might be done about my book, *Fossilized Customs.* It was causing them a great deal of trouble. It only takes one watchmen to cause 1000 to flee. It was not me at all, but Yahusha inside one of His Natsarim they were afraid of. When Truth sets us free from Nimrod's minions, Yahusha makes us ambassadors of His reign. Through us, He calls every person to repent because His reign is about to appear. The flesh does not, nor can it obey Yahuah's Turah without the calling, intervention, guidance, and assistance of Yahusha's Ruach ha Qodesh. Without realizing it, religious teachers are working against Yahusha by denying His Name, disobeying His Commandments,

ABOMINATION OF DESOLATION
IMAGE OF THE DESTROYER OF CIVILIZATION

The Hebrew concept of SHIQUTS is an image, translated **abomination**. The messenger Gabriel was sent to Danial about events in the future. An apocalyptic message concerning an **abomination of desolation** was referred to. As we search for this **destroyer of civilization**, we easily find what cannot be mistaken by anyone aware of history, or even the daily news. It will endure to the end.

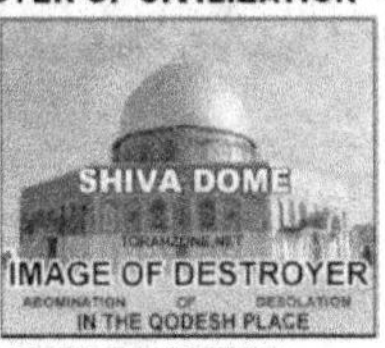

READER WILL UNDERSTAND - MT 24:15

Danial 12:11 describes the setting-up of an abomination, a common Hebrew interpretation for an idol, or form. Mt. 24:15 Refers to this text, Yahusha told us **the reader** would understand in the end times.

The **idolatrous form** associated with **desolation** is the Shiva dome, and it is set up (built) in a **qodesh place**: the Temple Mount.

The **destroyer** in the Hindu trinity is **Shiva**, whose **image** is primarily the **crescent**, associated with a **star**. The star represents his wife Shakti (avatar of Parvati).

The Shrines of Shiva the **destroyer** typically involve a **dome-shaped feature** (Shiva's phallus), the practice of circumambulation (walking around), a **shivalingam**, and a mat (a sacred space on which to bow to the idol). These Hindu features are expressed at the Shiva shrine at Mecca, and imitated at all other Muslim shrines around the world. As Christianity absorbed certain practices via Roman Sun worship, Islam reflects a Hindu version of the ancient Nimrod culture.

DOMED ARCHITECTURE

The Masonic connection to Shiva worship involves symbols such as the **crescent** and **star**, as well as the **dome designs** seen in the architecture of many religious and governmental buildings all over the Earth. The Masons worship a **great architect**, the original builder of the tower at Babel, **Nimrod**.

If we combine all these elements, the perfect candidate for the **abomination of desolation** (destroyer) is the Shiva shrine built on the Temple Mount by Muslims.

ISLAM:
DESTROYER OF CIVILIZATION
John Wesley on Islam:

"Ever since the religion of Islam appeared in the world, the espousers of it ... have been as wolves and tigers to all other nations, rending and tearing all that fell into their merciless paws, and grinding them with their iron teeth; that numberless cities are raised from the foundation, and only their name remaining; that many countries, which were once as the garden of God,

DOERS OF THE WORD
NOT HEARERS ONLY, DECEIVING YOURSELVES

When Yahusha returns, will He find amanah (steadfast obedience) on the Earth? Yes He will, and He is putting us to work in the harvest right now! We're Still Here Yahusha! We are doers of the Word, not hearers only. Those who think of themselves as Christians were originally known by a former label given to them by Yahusha when He said, "ANI HA GAFEN; ATAH HA NATSARIM."

Translated into English, it means, "I am the Vine; you are the NATSARIM," see Yn. 15:5

If you are doing the Word, or on the path to learning His Word, the adversary knows it. You will want to share this tract with Christian friends who do not yet know what Yahusha calls them.

Back To Our Hebrew Roots

Words mean important things. We were first known by a Hebrew word that started with the letter N: NATSARIM (Acts 24:5). 2000 years later, Yahusha's question at Luke 18 about finding AMANAH (belief, steadfast obedience, trust) on the Earth helps us see how decadent and misguided our walk has become. AMANAH (steadiness, obedience) is the Hebrew word used at Kabaquq 2:4, and quoted at Galatians 3:11, Romans 1:17, and Hebrews 10:38. This relates directly to Yn. 8:31-32: "If you abide (live by) in My Word, you are truly My talmidim, and you will know the Truth, and the Truth will set you free."

The prophet Kabaquq spoke of the time of the end, and told us so. Kabaquq 2:1-4: "I stand at my watch, and station myself on the watch-tower, and wait to see what He says to me, and what to answer when I am reproved. And Yahuah answered me and said, 'Write the vision and inscribe it on tablets, so that he who reads it runs. For the vision is yet for an appointed time, and it speaks of the end, and does not lie. If it lingers, wait for it, for it shall certainly come, it shall not delay. See, he whose being is not upright in him is puffed up. But the obedient one lives by his steadfastness (amanah).'"

If we live by every Word, we see how far the world, as well as Christian pastors.

SIGNS ALL AROUND US

N IS FOR NATSARIM
SHATAN KNOWS WHO HE IS AFTER
CHRISTIANS ARE CALLED
NASRANI BY ARABS
NOTSRIM BY YAHUDIM
NATSARIM BY ACTS 24:5

GRAFTING IN
DO NOT CONSIDER YOURSELF SUPERIOR TO OTHERS

RESTORATION OF TWO STICKS

Yekezqal (Ez.) 37 speaks of the House of Yahudah and the House of Yisharal as two sticks (or trees). The book pictured at right was so thrilling for me to read, my heart leaped within me with joy after just a few pages into it. Yahuah is about to do something that those who hear of it will feel their ears tingle. Kings will shut their mouths; they will see what they have not been told, and understand what they have not heard. (YashaYahu / Is. 52)

Yahuah scattered us, and promised to regather us from where He had scattered us among the foreigners. Yahuah scattered the tribes in order to bring deliverance to foreigners. YashaYahu (Is.) 49:6 and Acts 13:47 tells us why He mixed the tribes among all nations: to bring His deliverance to the ends of the Earth. Amos 9 verifies this. Now we see His plan is to awaken us to our heritage in the last days, and then re-gather us at the Second Exodus described at YirmeYahu 3. Yahuah has awakened hunters and fishers: "Therefore see, the Yomim (days) are coming, says Yahuah, when it is no longer said, Yahuah lives Who brought up the children of Yisharal from the land of Mitsrayim, but, Yahuah lives Who brought up the children of Yisharal from the land of the north and from all the lands where He had driven them. For I shall bring them back into their land I gave to their fathers. See, I am

sending for many fishermen, says Yahuah, and they shall fish them. And after that I shall send for many hunters, and they shall hunt them from every mountain and every hill, and out of the holes of the rocks." YirmeYahu / Jer. 16:14-16

Our teachers are the source of all our confusion; they run to teach, but Yahuah did not send them. There are divisive issues of many kinds based on bigotry, genealogy, and men's philosophies causing great disturbance among those being called out of idolatry, and struggling to be restored to favor. The only thing a person can offer to Yahuah is their obedience to His Torah, since all else is chaff.

Some sample content of tracts you can download free (first pages shown here).
Or get them all quickly; there are over 100 tracts on the AMBASSADISC digital library.
Each tract is 4 pages, and formatted to print double-sided on a single sheet of paper.

THE DAY OF YAHUAH

THE EAGLES ARE COMING
DO YOU KNOW WHO THEY ARE?

Mat 24:28, 29: "For wherever the dead body is, there the eagles shall be gathered together. And immediately after the distress of those days the sun shall be darkened, and the moon shall not give its light, and the stars shall fall from the heaven, and the powers of the heavens shall be shaken."

"WHOEVER CALLS UPON THE NAME OF YAHUAH WILL BE DELIVERED" - Yual (Joel) 2, Acts 2. The reason they will be delivered is:
THEY HAVE BEEN SEALED WITH THE NAME OF YAHUSHA, THE DELIVERER.
Our Owner places His Name on His property, so the REAPERS will not harm what belongs to Him.

Our Redeemer is on His way, and the fallen malakim know their time is short.

People believing in a pre-Trib rapture will make some adjustments in their expectations, and come to accept the reality unfolding around them. Most of them today are Sun-day Sabbath people, and many are becoming **Natsarim** * – end-time harvest workers.

Our most important work during the time of distress will be to help them be restored to the Covenant of Yahuah - His Torah - the message of AbYahu. (See Mal 4:1-6)

WITHOUT WARNING, ONE DAY THE SUN WILL SUDDENLY SHUT DOWN, AND IN A SHORT TIME THE ENTIRE SOLAR SYSTEM WILL BE IN DEEP DARKNESS. THE DAY OF OUR REDEMPTION WILL COME, AND WE CAN LOOK UP EXPECTANTLY. THE MESSENGERS WILL BE SENT TO REAP THE HARVEST OF THE EARTH FIRST. THEY WILL "GATHER" THE WEEDS TO BURN THEM. THEN, THOSE FOUND KEEPING THE COMMANDMENTS OF YAHUAH AND AWAITING THE BRIDEGROOM WILL BE GATHERED FOR THE WEDDING FEAST (SUKKOTH, TABERNACLES) AT THE COMING OF YAHUSHA. DO NOT BE AFRAID. COMFORT ONE ANOTHER WITH THESE WORDS.
*Acts 24:5

"But the Day of Yahuah shall come as a thief in the night, in which the heavens shall pass away with a great noise, and the elements shall melt with intense heat, and the earth and the works that are in it shall be burned up." - 2Pe 3:10

"And the present heavens and the Earth are treasured up by the same Word, being kept for fire, to a day of judgment and destruction of wicked men." - 2Pe 3:7

"And now, be wise, O sovereigns; be instructed, you rulers of the Earth. Serve Yahuah with fear, and rejoice with trembling. Kiss the Son, lest He be enraged, and you perish in the way, for soon His wrath is to be kindled. Blessed are all those taking refuge in Him." - Psa 2:10-12 (See also Acts 17:30-31)

page 1 of 4

KJV: A JABBERING LIP
AND A FOREIGN TONGUE

A "Black Swan Event" is a term used to describe an unforeseen event that comes as a surprise with major effects. It is impossible to predict, but with the benefit of hindsight it can be identified for what it is.

For over **400 years** the KJV has trained the entire world to speak the English language. **Now a prophecy is being fulfilled;** average people are learning the Hebrew Name of our Creator is Yahuah, not GOD or LORD. **Furthermore, the evidence of a huge conspiracy to hide the Name is exposed**

PUTTING THINGS IN ORDER

The first protestants remained Catholic, they only protested the head of the Kirche being the papacy. The **KJV** is an **Anglican Catholic** translation. The KJV was used to teach English to the whole world for 400 years. It was based on the Latin Vulgate, and now helps point out what was withheld from us. Truth is being restored, and tradition exposed. The famine of Yahuah's Word is ending as people are discovering the **Hebrew Name** of our Creator.

It is the **key of knowledge** withheld by those responsible for teaching all the nations the message of deliverance. The Scriptures are Hebrew in origin. The English language fulfils a prophecy at YashaYahu (Isaiah) 28:11 where it tells us Yahuah will speak to this people through a **jabbering lip** and a **foreign tongue** (language). Yahuah allowed the British colonies to flourish around the globe just as the printing press was invented. This spread the English language throughout the Earth, using the KJV to do so. Foreign students learned English by reading from the KJV. This training has lasted for 400-years. It prepared the world so all could understand the conspiracy to conceal the true Name. The famine is over for those who are hungry for the highest of all things: the **Word** and **Name** of Yahuah (Ps. 138:2).

KJV - EVIDENCE OF A CONSPIRACY
Translators hijacked the Name. For those who diligently seek the Truth, the tools are available to find the true Name of our Deliverer. **Translations** have hidden His Name from us, and anyone can see this by reading the preface of their **NIV**. The NIV admits substituting the Name with a "device," replacing it with the English word **LORD** in all capital letters. This was inherited from the word **DOMINUS** in the Latin Vulgate.

The English translations developed in several stages through men who were motivated for Yahuah's Word to be known by average people. In 1382, an English Catholic priest named **John Wycliffe** published an English translation of Jerome's Latin Vulgate. His extensive work laid the initial foundation for all the English translations that followed. Translations of Yahuah's Word into any language but Latin was met with deadly results. The translators and those helping them were killed, some having their bones exhumed and burned many years after

---

SUNDAY ✠ ORIGINS
WORSHIP OF THE RISING SUN IN SUN TEMPLES

The first day of each week is called Sunday, and is a counterfeit sabbath invented by Constantine. His edict in 321 called it the "day of the Sun." Sunday worship is proxy-worship of satan, the adversary. This practice began with Nimrod, who after being slain was worshipped as the Sun. The cross symbol represented the Sun and was called **Shammash** (at right). At Acts 7 Stephen addressed the Nasi and Great Sanhedrin (the president and council) about their persistence in worshipping the "host of heaven." Sun worship had also been going on in the days of Yekezqel, as it 10 states the zodiac (animals) were carved on the inside walls of Yahuah's Hekal. Yekezqel describes the Sun worship:

"And He said to me, 'You are to see still greater abominations which they are doing.' And He brought me to the door of the north gate of the House of Yahuah, and I saw women sitting there, weeping for Tammuz. Then He said to me, 'Have you seen this, O son of man? You are to see still greater abominations than these.' And He brought me into the inner court of the House of Yahuah. And there, at the door of the Hekal of Yahuah, between the porch and the altar, were about 25 men with their backs toward the Hekal of Yahuah and their faces toward the east, and they were bowing themselves eastward to the sun." Ez 8:13-16

W. H. Prescott's book on the History of the Conquest of Peru provides his eye-witness account of Sun worship:

"Eagerly they watched the coming of their deity, and, no sooner did his first yellow rays strike the turrets and loftiest buildings of the capital, than a shout of gratulation broke

INCENSE BURNER DEDICATED TO SHAMMASH

forth from the assembled multitude, accompanied by songs of triumph, and the wild melody of barbaric instruments, that swelled louder and louder as his bright orb rising above the mountain range towards the east shone in full splendor on his votaries.

After the usual ceremonies of adoration, a libation was offered to the great deity by the Inca, from a huge golden vase, filled with the fermented liquor of maize or of maguey, which, after the monarch had tasted it himself, he dispensed among his royal kindred. These ceremonies completed, the vast assembly was arranged in order of procession, and took its way towards the Qurikancha."

The Qurikancha (or the Hispanic form Coricancha) was a temple dedicated to the worship of Inti, the sun deity of the Inca. The Konark Sun Temple is at Konark, in Odisha, India. Rev. 2 describes these myths as the teachings of Izebel. The world has turned aside to myths just as Paul said at 2Tim 4. Babel's mythological patterns serve the dragon's purposes Dt 4:19 ", ... and lest you lift up your eyes to the heavens, and shall see the sun, and the moon, and the

---

HEBREW PHONOLOGY
THE STUDY OF THE SOUND OF A LANGUAGE

STOP! Hey, what's that sound? Everybody look what's going down . . . Yahuah tells us through the prophet ZefanYah they have done violence to His Torah. They also bent His language such that He promises to restore it: Zep 3:9: "For then I shall turn to the peoples a clean lip so that they all call on the Name of Yahuah to serve Him with one shoulder." YashaYahu 52:5: "Those who rule over them make them howl,' declares Yahuah, 'and My Name is despised all day continually."

To Yahuah, we sound like we're howling.

THE GOAL IS TO RESTORE YAHUAH'S NAME TO OUR SPEECH

A wise man once wrote:
"Men like the opinions to which they have been accustomed from their youth; they defend them, and shun contrary views; and this is one of the things that prevents men from finding truth, for they cling to the opinion of habit."
- Guide For The Perplexed, Moses Ben Maimon / Rambam (1135-1204)

TRANSLITERATION HYSTERIA
Transliterating transfers the letters of a language to another, preserving the exact sound of the original language.

People don't know what's happened or why when they see Abrahim spelled 'Avraham' or 'Ibrahim.' This Hebrew name begins with the letter ALEF, the letter "A." The first two letters are AB, not AV. Eber and Emmanual both begin with the letter AYIN, which may be rendered as an E or an A depending on the word. Often Eber and Emmanual are erroneously spelled Iber and Immanuel. On the Internet, people are spelling the city of peace "YAHrushalem" and making up names like "marYAH" and many others. They hear yara (shoot) or yerak (moon) and falsely perceive the sound of the Name, so they insert Yah into the word.

The confusion of Hebrew continues as if there are aftershocks from the mouthquake at the tower of Babel. The first two letters of the city of Yerushalayim are yod-resh, not

yod-hay, yet teachers are spelling it as if the Name "Yah" is in the word.

All this confusion is from a combination of reasons. Hebrew should be understood as the language (speech) of the man Eber. Yahuah's Word refers to Hebrew by the term EBRITH. As teachers attempt to teach Hebrew, the original **Hebrew** script is often ignored entirely, and they use the Aramaic script while calling it "modern Hebrew." The Aramaic script was inherited from Babel in the days of Nekem Yah (Nehemiah).

NIQQUD - VOWEL MARKS
Teachers use vowel marks invented by the Masoretes to cue readers how to sound the vowels in Hebrew words. They claim these symbols (invented in the 8th century) are necessary because "Hebrew has no written vowels" - but this is entirely false. The Name Yahuah is written in four vowels: yod-hay-uau-hay. Uttering the Name was forbidden during the Babylonian Captivity. The vowel-marks are intended to stop the proper utterance of the Name, cueing the reader to pronounce "adonai" in place of the actual Name. They admit this is so. To utter the Name aloud was (and still is) considered blasphemy, yet the niqqud distortions are the true blasphemy. This is confirmed by the fact that in 2008 a papal bull was issued that forbids the Name "Yahweh" in worship, song, or prayer.

Some sample content of tracts you can download free (first pages shown here). Or get them all quickly; there are over 100 tracts on the AMBASSADISC digital library. Each tract is 4 pages, and formatted to print double-sided on a single sheet of paper.

ALEF-TAU

The first and last letters of the Hebrew Alef-Beth are mysteriously placed near the Covenant Name (identity) of Yahuah throughout the Scriptures. It is an identity marker of the First and the Last, finally revealed by Yahusha ha'Mashiak as Himself at Rev. 1:8.

THE REVELATION OF YAHUSHA'S IDENTITY

The beast apparatus is the "world order" filled with deception for those who reject receiving a love for the Truth. For most of the past 2000 years, the influence of eastern mysticism and Gnostic "enlightenment" has dominated the western world. This *Gnosticism* has multiplied itself and is now seen *everywhere*, posing as the various forms of "religion," all posturing themselves to be the only "truth." At the core of them all is the worship of the "host of heaven" (Zodiac/Astrology), originating in Babel's worship of *Nimrod, Semiramis, and Tammuz*. This is the premise of Alexander Hislop's book, *The Two Babylons*. The false worship of the sun, moon, and constellations (Zodiac, zoo animals) manifests itself in the *three heads*, and sometimes *triple pairs of arms* depicted in statues.

Beads, flowers, nimbuses (haloes), ashes (note forehead of image at right), and meditation positions are just a few of the aspects of Babel's false worship. The majority of the "church fathers" were originally followers of *Manichaeism*, a religion founded by **Mani** (216-277CE).

Manichaeism was a major **Gnostic religion**, originating in Sassanid-era Babylonia.

Mani's Gnostic teachings about Yahusha became the pattern seen in many tenets of Christianity, adopted through the "church fathers." These pretenders are often referred to as "men of the cloth," wearing their special robes as we see with any other uniformed professional.

The people of Beroia (Acts 17) checked Scripture to validate everything they heard. Since that time, Gnostic beliefs were adopted, and it was taught that the Creator is THREE, not ONE as the *Shema* states. This has been promoted so well that *any who challenge that premise are regarded as heretics*. For a moment, let's think *outside that box* (prison, stronghold), and go with the working premise that the Creator is **ONE**, as He claims He is.

TRINITY CONFUSION

Since Yahusha declared that He and the Father are **one**, let's hypothetically take that statement at literally. If Yahuah entered into His physical world and *appeared* as one of us, that which we could see and touch of Him would be His "son" revealing Himself just as the opening words of Hebrews explain:

Heb 1:1-6: **"Alahim, having of old spoken in many portions and many ways to the fathers by the prophets, has in these last days spoken to us (by or as) the Son, whom He has appointed heir of all, through whom also He made the ages, Who being the brightness of the esteem and the <u>exact</u> representation of His substance, and sustaining all by the Word of His power, having made a cleansing of our sins through Himself, sat down at the right hand of the Greatness on high, having become so much better than the messengers, as He has inherited a more excellent Name than them. For to which of the messengers did He ever say, 'You are My Son, today I have brought You forth?' And**

IMAGE OF THE BEAST

CONSTANTINE & HIS UNIVERSALISM INITIATIVE

IMAGE OF THE BEAST
COMMON IN EVERY PLACE & TIME PERIOD

Sun worship was universalized during the reign of Constantine.
His creed is quoted in this document, and he ended it with his curse.

The dragon poisoned the waters (people) by mixing-in familiar symbols & customs. Sun-day, trinities, cruxes, pillars, haloes, statues, prayers to the dead using beads and candles are all from the Far East.

CONSTANTINE'S CREED:

"I renounce all customs, rites, legalisms, unleavened breads and sacrifices of lambs of the Hebrews, and all the other festivals of the Hebrews, sacrifices, prayers, aspirations, purifications, sanctifications, and propitiations, fasts and new moons, Sabbaths, superstitions, hymns and chants, observances. and assemblies. Absolutely everything Yahudi, every law, rite, and custom, and if afterwards I shall wish to deny and return to Yahudim superstition, or shall be found eating with Yahudim, or feasting with them, or secretly conversing and condemning the Christian religion instead of openly confuting them and condemning their vain faith, then let the trembling of Cain and the leprosy of Gehazi cleave to me, as well as the legal punishments to which I acknowledge myself liable. And may I be an anathema in the world to come, and may my soul be set down with satan and the devils."

Natsarim wishing to join this "holy community" were compelled to adopt a different set of rules and customs. All new members were to take this oath:
"I accept all customs, rites, legalism, and feasts of the Romans' sacrifices. Prayers, purifications with water, sanctifications by Pontificus Maximus (high priest of Rome), propitiations, and feasts, and

Some sample content of tracts you can download free (first pages shown here).
Or get them all quickly; there are over 100 tracts on the AMBASSADISC digital library.
Each tract is 4 pages, and formatted to print double-sided on a single sheet of paper.

Our enemy is not flesh and blood. When anyone awakens, their dreaming stops. The controller (beast) is losing, and has been on a downward spiral since Yahusha opened the eyes of His Natsarim.
Undirected knowledge of the existence of the controller isn't enough; only the Truth can set us free.

While we are still here, you can order directly from here: **torahzone.net**
Because we're in our 70's, we've also put the books on Amazon for international orders because they are printed near the person ordering them. Also, when Yahusha takes us, they will still remain available. Amazon prints and distributes over 70 percent of the world's books at the moment, and makes them available as eBooks as well.
We would love to ship directly for you, but as I said we can only do what we can do - Yahusha has reminded us to number our days, and as Eccl. 9:10 advises, what your hand finds to do, do it with all your might - you can do nothing from sheol, where you are going.

Remember the three words this book started out to teach you? The First Commandment identifies WHO we are to obey, and to have no other.

He's looking for His *obedient* ones, so let's listen to *Him*, and no one else.

We now know we cannot trust the translators and teachers of tradition.

In the Preface of the NASB, they admit the Name is most significant,
and it is inconceivable for anyone to think of not using the proper designation.
Then, they explain they did what they said is inconceivable:

The Proper Name of God in the Old Testament: In the Scriptures, the name of God is most significant and understandably so. It is inconceivable to think of spiritual matters without a proper designation for the Supreme Deity. Thus the most common name for deity is God, a translation of the Hebrew *Elohim*. The normal word for Master is Lord, a rendering of *Adonai*. There is yet another name which is particularly assigned to God as His special or proper name, that is, the four letters YHWH (Exodus 3:14 and Isaiah 42:8). This name has not been pronounced by the Jews because of reverence for the great sacredness of the divine name. Therefore, it was consistently pronounced and translated Lord. The only exception to this translation of YHWH is when it occurs in immediate proximity to the word Lord, that is, *Adonai*. In that case it is regularly translated God in order to avoid confusion.

𐤉𐤆𐤄𐤋𐤀 𐤄𐤅𐤄𐤉 𐤉𐤊𐤍𐤀
ANOKI YAHUAH ALAHIK
(I AM YAHUAH YOUR ALAH)

Yahusha will sing these words over us at His return. If you receive Him, you receive the One Who sent Him. He is Al Shaddai.

VIDEO LINKS (ACTIVE IN E-BOOK)

FOUNDATIONAL TEACHING:

What is The Purpose of Life?
Foundational Beliefs
Who Are The Natsarim
The First Natsarim Documentary
NATSARIM: HERETICS

THE TRUE NAME

The Name of Yahuah Study
Restoring The Key of Knowledge
When Stones Cry Out
Yahuah's Name Under Siege
The Name of Yahusha Study
SHORT VID: Say `YAH-HOO-AH'
SHORT VID: YAHUAH - yod-yah-uau-hay
SHORT VID: YAHUSHA - yod-hay-uau-shin-ayin
FULL SEMINAR: THE STONES CRY OUT

THE COVENANT:

The Everlasting Covenant
The Ten Commandments
Yahuah's Top Ten Instructions
FULL SEMINAR: RESTORATION
FULL SEMINAR: THE GOSPEL

DELIVERANCE:

Repentance
Immersion
SHORT VID: Immersion

THE SABBATH:

VIDEO: **The Reality Of The Sabbath**

What is permitted on the Sabbath?
LIVE SEMINAR: THE SABBATH - KEEP IT SET-APART
LIVE SEMINAR: THE SABBATH BREACH
LIVE SEMINAR: THE HEARTBEAT OF CREATION
APPOINTED TIMES TO OBSERVE:
Passover & Shabuoth for Children
Happy Anniversary Yahuah
Yahusha: The Lamb Legacy
Yahusha: The Passover
Yahusha: The Servant King
Yahusha: The Firstfruit
Jubilees / Shabuoth (Pentecost)
The Harvest Feasts
Yom Teruah (trumpets) 2011
Yom Teruah (trumpets) 2013
Yom Kafar (atonement) 2011
Yom Kafar (atonement) 2013
Sukkoth 2011
Simkat Torah (the joy) 2011
LIVE SEMINAR: THE SERVANT

LIVE SEMINAR: THE OBSERVANCES OF YAHUAH

END-TIME EVENTS:
Immortality & Consolidation of Global Powers
Aliens / UFOs / GMOs / D.U.M.Bs
The Samson Option
The Wheat & Darnel
The Day of Yahuah
The New Yerushalayim
The Lamps & Virgins
Eschatology & the Fourth Beast
The Two Witnesses
The Second Exodus
The Two Resurrections
LIVE SEMINAR: THE ESCHATON
LIVE SEMINAR: THE WAR IN HEAVEN
LIVE SEMINAR: WHITE ROBES
SHORT VID: Will You Be 'Left Behind'?
SHORT VID: A Higher Calling

NATSARIM LIVING:
The Transformation Process
Beginning Again as a Natsarim
Natsarim Dating & Marriage
Bedroom Behaviour & Sexuality
Living in a Disrespectful Society
The Test of a Servant
Hair on the head & Beards
The Storms of Life
Eating Kosher Food
Trusting Yahusha
Child-Rearing
Evil Spirits in our Homes
Money-Trading

Torah Behaviour
Our Common Deliverance
Real Witnessing is A Behaviour
RULES OF ENGAGEMENT FOR NATSARIM
SHORT VID: Praying To Spirits?
SHORT VID: The Pride of Life
LIVE SEMINAR: THE TEST
LIVE SEMINAR: THE SHEKINAH
LIVE SEMINAR: POSSESSION
LIVE SEMINAR: PERSECUTION
LIVE SEMINAR: THE REAL FINAL SOLUTION

TOPICS OF INTEREST:
Death and the Afterlife
Waymarks of the Lost Tribes
Ancient Vikings
Seven Wonders of the World
Is Yahukanon (John/Lazarus) Still Alive?
The Pope's Resignation 2013
Where is the Synagogue of Shatan?
Hypocrites Documentary
LIVE SEMINAR: EVOLUTION vs INTELLIGENT DESIGN
LIVE SEMINAR: DEATH - THE LAST ENEMY
SHORT VID: Science vs True Knowledge
SHORT VID: Is Hellfire Real???

MAJOR STRONGHOLDS:
The Lunar Sabbath Beast
Mother Nature & The Zodiac
Humanism / Olympic Games / Valentine's Day
Early Councils of Doom
The Asherah Curse
LIVE SEMINAR: Kabbala
LIVE SEMINAR: Toxic Torah / Supersessionism

LIVE SEMINAR: THE TRINITY
LIVE SEMINAR: HUMAN TRADITIONS
LIVE SEMINAR: SYNCRETISM
LIVE SEMINAR: APOSTASIA
LIVE SEMINAR: DOCTRINE OF DEMONS
LIVE SEMINAR: RACIAL IDENTITY
LIVE SEMINAR: EASTER - WHO IS SHE?
LIVE SEMINAR: WITCHCRAFT
LIVE SEMINAR: THE IMAGE OF THE BEAST
LIVE SEMINAR: IDENTIFYING WORMWOOD
SHORT VID: The Zodiac
SHORT VID: The Xmas Tree

SCRIPTURES TRANSLATION DISCUSSIONS:
The BYNV Project
The BYNV Completion
The King James Version
The Prophetic Books
LIVE SEMINAR: OUR BELOVED BROTHER PAUL

FAMILY FELLOWSHIP VIDEOS
MUSIC VIDEOS
YAHUSHA'S BODY SCRIPTURE STUDIES
FOSSILIZED CUSTOMS VIDEO-BOOK
SAMPLERS

Most people are taught fake, made-up names for our Creator. They practice adopted pagan rituals and embrace behavior our Messiah died to cover the penalty for doing such things. They eat ham, teach children to hunt eggs, erect trees, dance around poles, carve pumpkins, ignore the day of rest, and much more. Yahuah said, "My People Will Know My Name."
Draw near to Him, and you'll notice a very small number really know Him.

They say they know Him, but 1 Yahukanon (John) 3 is the perfect way to test them.
https://youtu.be/SIM5QrqEixY

The Creator's Name, and His Word, is known and practiced by "His People."
Outside are the dogs, those practicing a lie, and they are not His People.

POST SCRIPT

The Mark Of The Beast Is A Riddle

The solving of the riddle requires wisdom (see Prov. 1:6, Ps. 49:4).
Without wisdom, no one is able to solve the riddle at Rev. 13 that concerns "buying and selling."
Yahukanon's writings allude to a beast (behemoth), and the interpretation of the elements he describes are presented as a riddle to be solved.
He does not provide you with all the pieces to solve it, but points to how to find the missing components.
Revelation 13:16-17 relates this riddle to be associated with "buying and selling."
Here is wisdom: let him who has understanding perform the calculation. Look at all the components, then add wisdom, and you solve it easily.
Wisdom is Torah, and gives the simple the ability to solve riddles.
The reason few know how to solve the riddle is they have no regard for Torah.
There is a veil over their minds regarding *Shabath*.
The sign forever between Yahuah and His people.
fossilizedcustoms.com/mark.html

"My Aduni And My Alahim"

These words of Thomas are found at Yn. 20:28.

Philippians 2:10-11 has been veiled by the removal of the Name from translations.

Kurios / **Dominus** (Greek and Latin terms for LORD) were devices used to **replace** the Name of Yahuah (see they admit this in the Preface of your translation). It should read Every knee will bow and every tongue will admit that Yahuah is Yahusha ha Mashiak, to the esteem of the Father. He is one and the same essence as Abba.

Yahuah *is* Yahusha ha Mashiak, and at His first coming in the flesh, He reconciled mankind to Himself. At His second coming, He'll *stay forever*. He is Al Shaddai, the First and the Last (Rev. 1:8).

There's much, much more evidence in Scripture. Yahusha is omnipresent; can I get a witness?
http://fossilizedcustoms.com/omnipresence.html

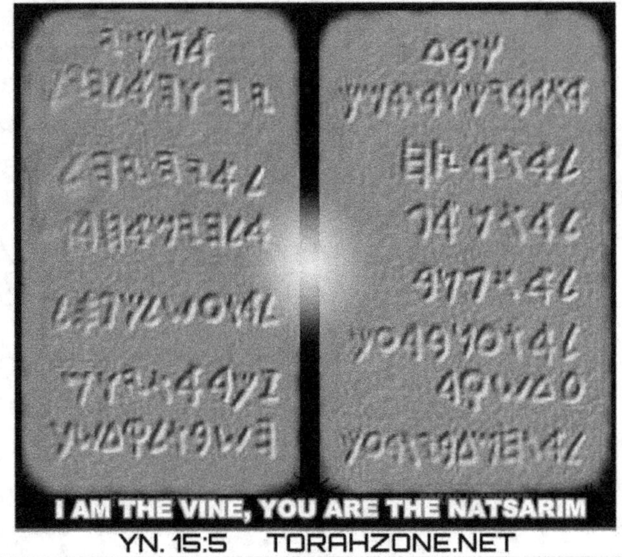

People have asked me, *"Why do you sell things to help teach people about Yahuah?"*
In other words, why don't you give everything away for free to all who want them? The answer is simple. One person can only do so much, but many can move mountains. With the limited resources of one person, little can be accomplished.
A flow of water turns the wheel of a mill. If the water stops, no grinding can happen.
The dragon would love me to stop doing what is working, deplete my resources, and starve to death.
Yahusha said what was whispered in the inner rooms would be shouted from the rooftops.
The Natsarim are crying-out the Name & Word.

My motivation to go to the lost in every possible way came from reading the words,

"Who will go for us?"

The BYNV Scriptures, books, and other items are manufactured and moved around the planet at great cost and effort. The Word conveys information that helps people to hear the Name of Yahuah, and know His Word. Psalm 102:18 tells us His Name was written long ago for a future generation to call on the Name.

The sons of Light need to be as shrewd as the sons of darkness, and not hide behind excuses to not print the Name above all names. The real value is in what Yahusha does in the human heart, not the paper, vinyl, or cloth that first made them look at His Name.

At **torahzone.net** we offer printable PDF's for free, but the website expense for us is not free. If the printing of flags, stickers, shirts, tracts, and books - and the shipping expense - were free, then many jobs would be lost as they all closed their doors, because the workers must be paid to feed themselves and pay for living expenses. I work many hours writing and packing orders, but rest according to the Commandment. The bookmarks with the Ten Commandments with letter charts on the back have gone into prisons, and studying them has changed the lives of prisoners. Why are they not free? The question being asked is non-sequitur, because it needs to be addressed to the owners of sawmills, farms, truck drivers, and large producers of the materials that go into the things we "sell."

Romans 10:14-15:

"How then shall they call on Him in whom they have not believed? And how shall they believe

*in Him of whom they have not heard? And how
shall they hear without one proclaiming? And
how shall they proclaim if they are not sent?"*
Besorah Of Yahusha Natsarim Version (BYNV)

Man's rule is coming to an end very soon, so all
men everywhere must repent (Acts 17).

BARUK HABA BASHEM YAHUAH
The world is now fully immersed in the Information
Age. Ignorance is no longer an excuse.
Yahuah instructed kings to write the Torah in their
own hand, and keep it with him at all times, and
read it everyday in order to respect Yahuah, and not
think of himself as better than those he rules over
(Dt. 17).
The first use of the form YAHUSHA is found at
Numbers 13:16, when Mushah changed the name
of HUSHA (hay-uau-shin-ayin) to YAHUSHA by
adding a yod to the beginning of his name. HUSHA
means deliverer, but by adding the one letter yod
the name transformed to the meaning "I am your
deliverer." Used as a proper noun, we find it used in
the TaNak 216 times.
https://biblehub.com/interlinear/numbers/13-16.htm
There is a new Ruler on His way very soon, and His
ambassadors remember what He said, and we are
telling the whole world. Teach His Name (Yahuah),
and guard everything we were commanded to obey
(Ten Words, Decalogue). He did not call us
"Christians," but said this: "I am the Vine, you are
the Natsarim." He said we would not see Him again
until we say, **"BARUK HABA BASHEM YAHUAH."**
We are saying it, so Google that phrase, and
prepare yourself.

To The Evolutionist
Academia generally prohibits the discussion of creation, and promotes evolutionary ideas. They assume life randomly evolved due to the right conditions over very long periods of time.
The "soup-starter" approach to the existence of life assumes there's no designer.
To seriously consider the possibility there is a designer leads to the stress of cognitive dissonance. To remain sane, one must keep their blinders firmly in place and ignore massive amounts of evidence on every scale. The human eye has both design and a purpose.
There is no evidence of any non-functioning eyes that led to the first fully-functioning eye. The failures that led to the the light bulb were many, yet not nearly as complex as the human eye.
Edison once said the light bulb was an invention (or design) with 1,000 steps. To ignore the intricate designs evident in everything around us and still assume they assembled themselves to serve no purpose without a designer is a form of delusion. Reality does not need to justify itself with an explanation.
Out of a whirlwind, the Designer asked Ayub,
"Where were you when I laid the foundations of the Arets? Declare it, if you have understanding." (Ayub 38:4, BYNV)

BYNU 𐤉𐤄𐤅𐤄 𐤉𐤄𐤅𐤔𐤏 RESTORED NAMES

BESORAH of YAHUSHA NATSARIM VERSION

LETTER STUDY CHART

LATIN		HEBREW	ARAMAIC			GREEK	
A	alef	𐤀	א	1	ox	alpha	A
B	beth	𐤁	ב	2	house	beta	B
G	gimel	𐤂	ג	3	camel	gamma	Γ
D	daleth	𐤃	ד	4	door	delta	Δ
H	hay	𐤄	ה	5	window	hoi	H
U	uau	𐤅	ו	6	hook	upsilon	Y
Z	zayin	𐤆	ז	7	weapon	zeta	Z
CH	heth	𐤇	ח	8	fence	(h)eta	H
T	teth	𐤈	ט	9	winding	theta	Θ
Y	yod	𐤉	י	10	hand	iota	I
K	kaph	𐤊	כ	20	bent hand	kappa	K
L	lamed	𐤋	ל	30	goad	lambda	Λ
M	mem	𐤌	מ	40	water	mu	M
N	nun	𐤍	נ	50	fish	nu	N
S	samek	𐤎	ס	60	prop	xei	Ξ
E/A	ayin	𐤏	ע	70	eye	omega	Ω
P	pe	𐤐	פ	80	mouth	pei	Π
TS	tsadee	𐤑	צ	90	hook	zeta	Z
Q	koph	𐤒	ק	100	needle eye	chi	X
R	resh	𐤓	ר	200	head	rho	P
SH	shin	𐤔	ש	300	tooth	sigma	Σ
T	tau	𐤕	ת	400	mark	tau	T

BYNU - A HEBREW-ROOTS TRANSLATION

THE ORDER OF THE BOOKS IMPROVES UNDERSTANDING

TORAH INSTITUTE

TORAHZONE.NET

NOTES: